The 500 Hidden Secrets of
GHENT

INTRODUCTION

This is a guide to the Ghent that almost no one knows. It tells you about the undiscovered chapels where you might be the only visitor, the cool coffee bars that play the best music and the hidden parks that are no bigger than a back garden. The book doesn't tell you everything there is to see. There are already guide books and websites that cover the familiar tourist places. This book goes one step further and lists the places the author would recommend to a friend who wanted to discover the real Ghent.

Here you will find the 5 best places to eat frites when hunger strikes, the 5 museums that no one should miss and the 5 coolest cycle routes out of town. The aim is to take the reader to the unexpected places that are different in some way from the normal tourist destinations. With this book tucked in your pocket, you can set out to find the most unexpected view of Ghent, the best place to find a snack at 2am, and the most romantic place to drink a cocktail.

This book also takes you to some of the strangest places in Ghent, like the vineyard hidden behind a high wall, the museum of madness and the network of canalside trails. It reveals a secret Indian restaurant hidden behind the sign La Bella Italia and a wallpaper shop that hasn't changed in 50 years. You do not have to do everything listed in the book, but you are urged at the very least to drink a Gruut beer in one of the 5 best bars, eat at one of the 5 best vegetarian restaurants, and watch a film in one of the 5 best small cinemas. If you do so, you will begin to understand one of the most undiscovered cities in Europe.

HOW TO USE THIS BOOK?

This book contains 500 things you need to know about Ghent in 100 different categories. Some are places to visit. Others are random bits of information. The aim is to inspire, not to cover the city from A to Z.

The places listed in the guide are given an address, a district and a number. The district and number allow you to find the locations on the maps at the beginning of the book. The maps are not detailed enough to navigate around the city, but you can pick up an excellent free city map at the Ghent tourist office, Sint-Veerleplein 5.

You need to bear in mind that cities change all the time. The chef who hits a high note one day can be uninspiring on the day you happen to visit. The hotel ecstatically reviewed in this book might suddenly go downhill under a new manager. The bar considered one of the 5 best places for live music might be empty on the night you visit.

This is obviously a highly personal selection. You might not always agree with it. If you want to leave a comment, recommend a bar or reveal your favourite secret place, you can contact the publisher at info@lusterweb.com.

THE AUTHOR

Derek Blyth has lived in Belgium for more than 20 years. As a journalist, he has explored almost every corner of the country. Formerly editor-in-chief of the Brussels English-language weekly *The Bulletin*, he has written several books on the Low Countries, including *Brussels for Pleasure* and *Flemish Cities Explored*. He also gives guided tours in Brussels, Antwerp and Ghent.

In 2012, he published a guide to *The 500 Hidden Secrets of Brussels*. An instant bestseller, it was widely praised in the press for showing people a side of the city they never knew existed. He went on to produce a guide to *The 500 Hidden Secrets of Antwerp* in 2013. Both guides are illustrated with photographs by Joram Van Holen that capture the authentic spirit of these cities.

The author has spent many years exploring Ghent. He eats and drinks and shops for clothes in Ghent. He has taken countless friends to STAM and Huis Colette and the deserted waterside walk along Visserij. He loves Ghent because it is stubbornly different and endlessly interesting.

The author is immensely grateful to the many Ghent people who have shared their secrets with him, especially Lisa Bradshaw of Flanders Today, Nathalie Dumon of the Ghent tourist office, Guy Dupont of the city archives, photographer and journalist Melanie Devrieze, local entrepreneur Koen Phlips, blogger Gudrun Rombaut, digital designer Fredo De Smet, PR specialist Amaury Van Kenhove, Bart van Aken of Paard van Troje, Hilde Peleman of Copyright, and Hadewijch Ceulemans of Luster. He also thanks Mary Maclure for joining him on some long walks in Ghent in search of the perfect place that no one knows about.

GHENT

overview

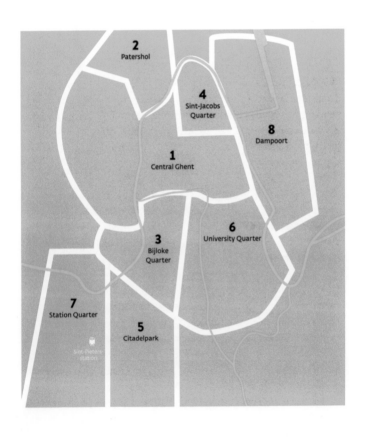

2 Patershol

4 Sint-Jacobs Quarter

8 Dampoort

1 Central Ghent

3 Bijloke Quarter

6 University Quarter

7 Station Quarter

5 Citadelpark

Sint-Pieters-
station

Map 1
CENTRAL GHENT

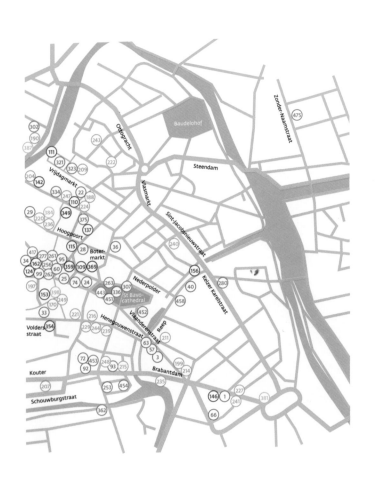

Map 2
PATERSHOL

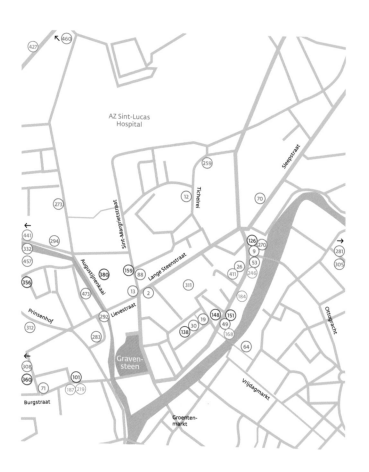

Map 3

BIJLOKE QUARTER

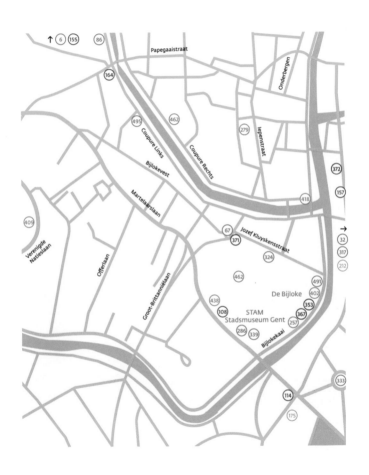

Map 4
SINT-JACOBS QUARTER

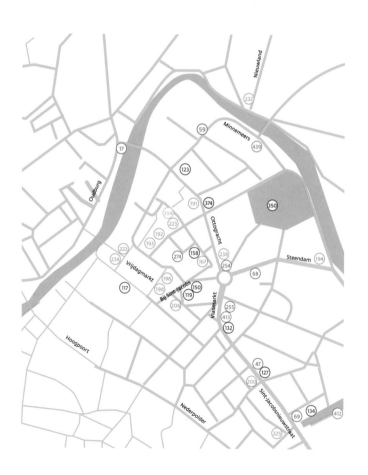

Map 5
CITADELPARK

Map 6
UNIVERSITY QUARTER

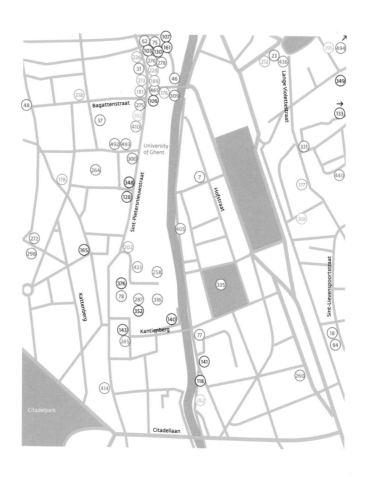

Map 7
STATION QUARTER

Map 8
DAMPOORT

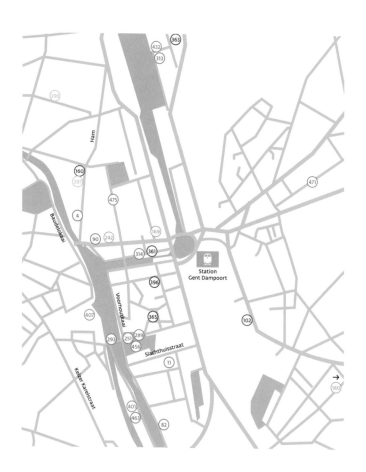

JOOST ARIJS

100 PLACES
TO EAT GOOD FOOD

The 5 best restaurants for
NEW FLEMISH COOKING

1 **DE VITRINE**
Brabantdam 134
Central Ghent ①
+32 (0)9 336 28 08
www.de-vitrine.be

Acclaimed Flemish chef Kobe Desramaults creates sensational menus based on the freshest seafood from Zeeland and the finest cuts of meat. He currently thrills his customers in a tiny bistro hidden behind a former butcher's shop near the city's red light district.

2 **J.E.F.**
Lange Steenstraat 10
Patershol ②
+32 (0)9 336 80 58
www.j-e-f.be

No name. No menu. Jason Blanckaert and his partner Famke run the most discreet foodie restaurant in town. But there is nothing simple about Blanckaert's cooking, which involves local seasonal food served in unexpected ways.

3 **VRIJMOED**
Vlaanderenstraat 22
Central Ghent ①
+32 (0)9 279 99 77
vrijmoed.be

Michael Vrijmoed opened this stylish restaurant in a handsome Ghent town house in 2012. It has a sober interior with bare wood floorboards, white walls and starched tablecloths. The food is simply stunning. Try the seafood dish served with smoked eel, Granny Smith apples, fennel, lemon and Japanese dashi. But first you have to book a table, which can be difficult.

4 PUBLIEK

Ham 39
Dampoort ⑧
+32 (0)9 330 04 86
www.publiekgent.be

Bare brick walls. Vintage chairs from an old school refectory. Olly Ceulenaere's new restaurant may look austere, but the food is anything but plain. The chef worked in some of the best kitchens in the country before opening this restaurant in 2014. He creates sublime menus that are constantly surprising.

5 NATURELL

Jan Breydelstraat 10
Central Ghent ①
+32 (0)9 279 07 08
www.naturell-gent.be

Lieven Lootens opened a new concept restaurant on the Leie waterfront in 2014 where his aim is to provide a theatrical dining experience that stimulates all the senses. Lootens takes time to find the freshest ingredients in the region and is especially skilled at turning humble local vegetables like the cabbage into something really special on the plate.

2 J.E.F.

The 5
COOLEST PLACES
TO EAT

---

6 **VOLTA.**
Nieuwe Wandeling 2b
Bijloke Quarter ③
+32 (0)9 324 05 00
www.volta-gent.be

This striking restaurant is located in the vast turbine hall of a former power station on the edge of the old town. The tiled floor and bare brick walls give the interior a stark industrial look. Olly Ceulenaere worked here before he moved on to open his own place, leaving young chef Davy De Pourcq to run the kitchen. He cooks inventive dishes featuring fresh vegetables grown in a garden just outside Ghent.

7 **DE SUPERETTE**
Guldenspoorstraat 29
University Quarter ⑥
+32 (0)9 278 08 08
www.indewulf.be

The acclaimed chef Kobe Desramaults has created a hip new bakery and restaurant in a quiet back street of Ghent. Opened in 2014, it occupies a former corner store called Superette Edwin. Desramaults has transformed the interior into a striking loft space with rough brick walls, vintage furniture and a wood-burning bread oven. You can pick up a round sourdough loaf at the counter, or sit down for breakfast, lunch or dinner. The kitchen crew produce some inspired cooking, but it is quite pricey.

8 JOUR DE FETE

Gustaaf Callierlaan 233
Citadelpark ⑤
+32 (0)9 233 66 45
restaurantjourdefete.be

This striking restaurant moved in 2013 to the new Zebra complex in southern Ghent. Local politicians and academics bring their guests here to show them Ghent at its most inspiring. The interior has coloured wall tiles and a large concave window looking out onto a secluded terrace. The lunch menu is simple and cheap, while more sophisticated cooking happens in the evening.

9 UNCLE BABE'S BURGER BAR

Sluizekensstraat 2
Patershol ②
+32 (0)9 278 89 19

This friendly burger bar feels like an American roadside diner. It has big glass windows looking out on a busy traffic intersection and a playlist that favours 1950s songs. The staff are charming and bring glasses of water to the table as soon as you have sat down. The burgers are made with the best meat and served in a metal serving dish along with chunky wedge potatoes. Open most nights until 2 am.

10 OAK

Hoogstraat 167
Central Ghent ①
+32 (0)9 353 90 50
www.oakgent.be

Marcelo Ballardin spent time in Heston Blumenthal's kitchen before setting up his own restaurant in Ghent in 2014. The young Italian-Brazilian chef has perfected a cooking style that combines innovative ideas with the freshest ingredients. The relaxed modern interior makes the perfect setting for this style of contemporary cooking.

The 5 best restaurants to
EAT LIKE A LOCAL

---

11 **HET GOUDEN HOOFD**
Slachthuisstraat 96
Dampoort ⑧
+32 (0)487 20 65 01
www.hetgoudenhoofd.be

The old sign still hangs outside Het Gouden Hoofd (The Golden Head) dating from the time when the building was occupied by a meat wholesaler. The interior still has a raw industrial look, including bare brick walls and white tiles, while the tables, lamps and old school posters come from secondhand shops near the Sint-Jacobskerk. The cooking is based on traditional Belgian recipes everyone enjoys, like rabbit with prunes, while the beer list is dotted with interesting local specialities.

12 **DE STOKERIJ**
Tichelrei 2a
Patershol ②
+32 (0)9 279 95 85
www.destokerij-gent.be

This friendly brasserie owned by two brothers occupies a striking whitewashed building that was formerly a gin distillery. The interior has a rough edge, with bare brick walls and a big iron chimney. The cooking style is robust, featuring meaty Flemish classics such as *stoverij* (Flemish stew) and steaks done in various ways.

13 **DE LIEVE**

Sint-Margrietstraat 1
Patershol ②
+32 (0)9 223 29 47
www.eetkaffee-delieve.be

This relaxed, friendly place on the edge of the Patershol has been around since 1984. The handwritten menu lists old Flemish favourites like *stoofvlees* (Flemish stew), *konijn met pruimen* (rabbit with prunes) and steak served with fries, alongside unusual local specialities you might want to try once, such as *pens* (tripe). It has a homely Flemish atmosphere which makes it popular with homesick students. But it is only open from Monday to Friday.

14 **CAFÉ THEATRE**

Schouwburgstraat 5
Central Ghent ①
+32 (0)9 265 05 50
www.cafetheatre.be

This is a grand brasserie located in a corner building near the opera house. Some say it only recruits women who look like fashion models, but perhaps that is a local myth. You come here in the morning to drink a coffee and read the newspaper. Or you drop in for a quick bite at lunchtime. The *garnaalkroketten* (shrimp croquettes) are among the best in town.

15 **'T OUD CLOOSTER**

Zwartezustersstraat 5
Central Ghent ①
+32 (0)9 233 78 02
www.toudclooster.be

This dark, candlelit restaurant is a romantic place to spend a rainy winter evening. Formerly a monastery, it is furnished with long wooden tables, statues of Catholic saints and stained glass windows. The kitchen produces some solid Flemish cooking, including a tasty Ghent stew simmered in dark Chimay beer.

The 5 best restaurants for
ITALIAN FOOD

---

16 AL CASTELLO

Geldmunt 2
Central Ghent ①
+32 (0)9 223 89 01
www.al-castello.be

Ghent has countless Italian restaurants, but this is probably the most authentic. The interior is sober, even austere, but that is just like Italy. The father cooks. The sons serve. Order the *spaghetti vongole* if you want to eat well. Sometimes you will hear shouts from the kitchen, or occasionally the owner bursts into song. But this just adds to the charm of the place.

17 APERTO CHIUSO

Sleepstraat 82
St-Jacobs Quarter ④
+32 (0)9 233 72 64

Look out for the front end of a Fiat 500 and a large map of Italy in the window. Locals love this little Italian restaurant, so you really have to book a table. The staff are friendly (but occasionally overstretched) and the food that comes out of the open kitchen is authentic and delicious.

18 VIVA LA PUGLIA

Sint-Lievenspoort-
straat 224
University Quarter ⑥
+32 (0)476 20 22 45
www.lapuglia.be

This friendly trattoria is located in a quiet neighbourhood far from the tourist haunts. It is a very traditional Italian place. The interior is sober, but the cooking is authentic. Try the *scaloppini piccata* if you need to be convinced.

19 IN BOCCA LUPO

Corduwaniers-
straat 63
Patershol ②
+32 (0)9 224 25 42

This authentic Italian restaurant is located in a restored building in the Patershol district. The white walls and oak beams create a warm, rustic feel. The kitchen cooks simple Italian dishes such as *spaghetti vongole* and *saltimbocca*. But that is sometimes all you ask of a restaurant.

20 EAT LOVE PIZZA

Ajuinlei 10
Central Ghent ①
+32 (0)479 87 93 87
www.eatlove.be

Valentina Gatti's father ran a pizza restaurant. She started out as a lifestyle journalist but one day decided to follow in her father's footsteps. She created this cool place with sustainable wood furniture and then brought in the Ghent graphic artist Eva Mouton to draw a quirky mural at the entrance. The Italian chefs who work here create those thin pizzas they serve in Naples, but they add unusual toppings like truffles or turnip. The only problem here is that the cooking can be very slow.

The 5 most
ROMANTIC
RESTAURANTS

---

21 THE HOUSE OF ELIOTT

Jan Breydelstraat 36
Central Ghent ①
+32 (0)9 225 21 28
thehouseofeliott.be

Now this has to be the strangest restaurant in Ghent. It gets its name from a nostalgic British TV drama series set in a Parisian fashion house. Inside it is filled with mementoes of Old Paris including a mannequin dressed in a Chanel dress. An Edith Piaf songs plays in the background to complete the mood. You may not expect great cooking in such a place, but you could not be more wrong. The kitchen specialises in lobster which is cooked in several different ways. And the friendly owner pours you a little glass of something as you leave.

22 MARCO POLO

Serpentstraat 11
Central Ghent ①
+32 (0)9 225 04 20

Young couples love this friendly Italian trattoria located in a narrow cobbled street filled with little lights after dark. The interior is plain, with bare brick walls, intimate wooden tables and red candles. The chef believes in slow cooking with organic ingredients, so you may have a long wait before anything edible arrives on the table.

23 FAIM FATALE

Zuidstationstraat 14
University Quarter ⑥
+32 (0)9 269 04 48
www.faimfatale.be

This is a charming little restaurant located in a 19th-century town house with an open fire in the winter. The chef comes up with creative dishes using unexpected ingredients. There is even a little garden at the back for summer evenings.

24 DE FOYER

Sint-Baafsplein 17
Central Ghent ①
+32 (0)9 234 13 54
www.foyerntgent.be

Here is a beautiful brasserie hidden away on the first floor of a 19th-century theatre. The interior has old wood-panelled walls, neat black tables and potted palms. The kitchen comes up with a different menu each month based on traditional Belgian and French recipes.

25 DE RECHTVAARDIGE RECHTERS

Sint-Baafsplein 23
Central Ghent ①
+32 (0)9 224 31 09
www.derechters.be

This relaxed Flemish brasserie faces the Cathedral where the Van Eyck altarpiece hangs and takes its name from a panel that was stolen in 1934 and never recovered. The kitchen offers traditional Flemish dishes such as the popular *garnaalkroketten* (shrimp croquettes) and a delicious *stoverij* made with beef stewed in dark Westmalle dubbel and flavoured with sharp Tierenteyn mustard.

The 5 most authentic
ASIAN RESTAURANTS

---

26 RAMEN

Oudburg 51
Patershol ②
+32 (0)472 33 72 36
www.eetramen.be

We love this tiny Japanese noodle bar designed by the Ghent firm Studio Simple. Simple it is. The menu is written on white tiled walls. The customers perch at the counter eating out of big porcelain bowls. But the people in the tiny kitchen create sublime dishes like ramen noodle soup and the little filled dumplings that the Japanese call *gyoza*.

27 RIZ D'OR

Sint-Michielsstraat 10
Central Ghent ①
+32 (0)9 233 26 43

This small restaurant has been run by a Vietnamese couple since 1983. The woman cooks. The man serves. The interior is rather old-fashioned, but the food is delicious. The menu lists 12 different dishes including a vegetarian option. Students like this place because it is so cheap.

28 TOKYO SUSHI

Botermarkt 10
Central Ghent ①
+32 (0)9 233 44 12
www.tokyosushi.be

This friendly Asian restaurant has an odd interior that combines Flemish and Japanese elements. But the food on the plate is authentic Asian style. You can eat delicious sushi dishes served on wooden boards along with Thai curries and other Asian specialities.

29 AMATSU

Hoogpoort 29
Central Ghent ①
+32 (0)484 56 76 77
www.amatsu.be

This sober Japanese restaurant is located in a large town house near the Stadhuis. Everything here is fresh and beautifully presented. The owner comes from China but he has recruited a sushi chef from Japan who spent several years studying the art of serving raw fish. The result is close to perfection.

30 LE BAAN THAI

Corduwaniers-
straat 57
Patershol ②
+32 (0)9 233 21 41

This beautiful Thai restaurant occupies a handsome red mansion on a cobbled lane in the Patershol district. The interior is decorated in a warm tropical style with gilt mirrors, ornaments and orchids. The kitchen produces fragrant Thai dishes, including a spicy prawn soup with lemon and a noodle salad with minced pork and prawns.

30 LE BAAN THAI

The 5 best
DELICATESSENS

31 TRATTORIA DELLA MAMMA

Sint-Pieters-
nieuwstraat 36
University Quarter ⑥
+32 (0)9 234 17 01
*www.trattoriadella
mamma.be*

This is a friendly Italian delicatessen where you can pick up tasty dishes to take away like *zucchini ripiene* or *parmigiana melanzane*. But we prefer to sit in the back where there are a few tables covered with red and white checked cloths. The cooking is authentic Italian style, served with a basket of bread and a robust red wine. On summer days, a few tables are squeezed onto the pavement to create an even more authentic Italian mood.

32 WICKERHOFF

Nederkouter 135
Central Ghent ①
+32 (0)9 223 43 57
www.wickerhoff.be

Robert Wickerhoff has run a sophisticated delicatessen in the heart of Ghent for more than 25 years. He makes a range of take away meals using the best fish and meat he can find, along with delicious pâtés which he wraps carefully in thick paper. He recently acquired the building next door where he serves meals based on his favourite recipes. The secret garden at the back is a magical spot for a summer lunch.

33 AULA

Voldersstraat 24
Central Ghent ①
+32 (0)9 225 05 14
www.slagerij-aula.com

This delicatessen lies in the heart of Ghent opposite the Aula where university ceremonies are held. It is an upmarket food shop with quality meats, cheeses and imported specialities. You can also eat here perched on a stool at the lunch counter while the two chefs work in the open kitchen. Try their chicken salad with a glass of crisp white wine.

34 KOOKPUNT

Cataloniëstraat 3
Central Ghent ①
+32 (0)9 223 30 40
www.kook-punt.be

This old building was home to a hip restaurant for 28 years. But the restaurant closed down in 2013 to make way for a stylish delicatessen. You can pick up delicious salads, sandwiches and lunch bags, along with some imported specialities like Fentimans Tonic Water.

35 TOULOUSE

Koningin Elisabethlaan 41
Station Quarter ⑦
+32 (0)9 242 02 49
traiteurtoulouse.be

This beautiful new deli opened in 2013 close to Sint-Pieters Station. You can pick up tasty takeaway dishes here based on French and Belgian recipes. The shop also sells smart cardboard lunchboxes containing soup, a sandwich and a drink.

The 5 best places for
VEGETARIAN FOOD

---

36 DE WAREMPEL
Zandberg 8
Central Ghent ①
+32 (0)9 224 30 62
de.warempel.be

This restaurant occupies an old medical supplies shop that still has the old name above the door. Hidden down a quiet side street, it is a rather sober place with yellow ochre walls and heavy green tablecloths. You don't get much choice here, but it is always tasty.

37 PACHA MAMA
Jan-Baptist
Guinardstraat 9
University Quarter ⑥
+32 (0)9 330 33 35

Here is a relaxed vegetarian restaurant in the university quarter decorated with bare wood floors and white walls. The food is fresh and full of flavour, although the choice is limited. The kitchen does soup, salad and a dish of the day. You order at the counter and then find a table.

38 AVALON
Geldmunt 32
Central Ghent ①
+32 (0)9 224 37 24
restaurantavalon.be

This appealing vegan restaurant is overlooked by the grey stone walls of the Gravensteen. It's a welcoming place occupying several small rooms, including an intimate former kitchen with gleaming Dutch tiles on the walls. The chef cooks imaginative dishes using fresh vegetables, grains and fruit grown on organic farms in the Flemish Ardennes.

39 DE APPELIER

Citadellaan 47
Citadelpark ⑤
+32 (0)9 221 67 33
www.deappelier.be

This vegetarian restaurant is located in a 19th-century town house on the edge of the university quarter. It has been around since 1980. You can choose soup, a salad or a vegetarian dish of the day, while children get to choose the vegetables they want to eat. The back garden is a beautiful spot to eat in the summer.

40 KOMKOMMERTIJD

Reep 14
Central Ghent ①
+32 (0)9 269 02 10
www.komkommertijd.be

A narrow passageway leads into this large restaurant covered with a glass roof. It's fairly basic, like a school canteen. You serve yourself at the counter and clear away the plates after you have eaten. The food is cheap and wholesome, making it popular with students on a tight budget.

39 DE APPELIER

The 5 best places for
CHEAP EATS

---

41 LA BELLA ITALIA

Gebroeders Vande-
veldestraat 8
Central Ghent ⓘ
+32 (0)9 330 85 19

This place looks like a simple Italian restaurant serving the usual range of pizzas you get everywhere. But it's not that simple. La Bella Italia is an Indian family restaurant where you can eat exceptionally tasty dishes such as Chicken Tandoori or Murgh Biryani. Or you order pizza. The interior is not particularly special, but it has a certain charm that many find irresistible.

42 BALLS & GLORY

Jakobijnenstraat 6
Central Ghent ⓘ
+32 (0)486 67 87 76
www.ballsnglory.be

The Flemish TV chef Wim Ballieu creates his handcrafted meatballs using pork from his grandfather's pig farm in West Flanders combined with minced beef and herbs. He serves them in a white bun filled with stoemp (mashed potato and carrot). They are served in a cardboard box along with a free jug of water. You can eat them sitting at a long window table in a cool industrial space.

42 BALLS & GLORY

43 DE BLAUWE KIOSK

Kouter
Central Ghent ⓘ
www.deblauwekiosk.be

One of the last kiosks in Ghent was carefully restored and painted blue in 1990. It no longer sells newspapers, but instead offers a plate of six oysters with a glass of white wine during the weekly flower market on Sunday morning.

44 KETCHUP

Hoornstraat 1
Central Ghent ⓘ

This bright little burger bar is decorated with rows of Heinz ketchup bottles. The menu lists 11 meat burgers and three veggie options. They cook the burgers to order on an open grill and serve them with tasty *frietjes*. It takes time (you wait upstairs in the little eating area until your name is called) but the end result is so much better than a fast food joint.

45 PURE DAPHNÉ

Gebroeders Vande-
veldestraat 3
Central Ghent ⓘ
+32 (0)9 278 22 80
www.puredaphne.be

Daphné Aers's gourmet croquette bar is one of the coolest eating spots in Ghent. The interior is decorated with a 19th-century tiled floor, shiny wood tables and a few comfortable leather armchairs. You will need to have things explained, as the croquettes come in various sizes. They are served with unusual fillings such as goats' cheese, octopus or tuna, accompanied by a little bowl of nibbles, brown bread, two types of sauce and a generous salad. Pure pleasure.

The 5 best places for
SOUP AND SANDWICHES

---

46 SOEPPLUS
Lammerstraat 33
University Quarter ⑥
+32 (0)9 223 16 88
+32 (0)475 91 84 58
www.soepplus.be

Here is the perfect place for a thick pea soup served with a hunk of brown bread. Barbara Defour makes three different soups every morning down in the basement of her cool white soup bar. She also creates delicious salads and tasty sandwiches. Everyone loves this place, so it can get busy at lunchtime. But there are two large rooms upstairs with wood floors, boxes of toys and a view of the river.

47 VENTURA
Sint-Jacobs-
nieuwstraat 25
St-Jacobs Quarter ④
+32 (0)9 335 47 59
+32 (0)479 54 20 27
www.linoventura.be

This smart soup bar in the St-Jacobs Quarter has the look of an old Flemish kitchen. It has a typical Belgian tiled floor, tiny wooden tables for two and vases filled with fresh roses. The two soups of the day are kept warm in large black cooking pots on the counter, while the blackboard lists various sandwiches made with thick brown bread.

48 VERLORENKOST

Nederkouter 134
University Quarter ⑥
+32 (0)9 329 59 34
www.verlorenkost.be

This is a friendly sandwich bar run by a young couple who take care to work with the freshest ingredients. You can sit on stools at the front looking out on the trams or hide away upstairs. A long list of options is chalked on a blackboard. Some have unexpected touches, like the *Broodje Verlorenkost* – a sliced baguette filled with fried mince, raw chicory, chives dressing and a dash of red curry. The sandwiches are made to order so it can sometimes be slow.

49 SOUPLOUNGE

Zuivelbrugstraat 6
Patershol ②
+32 (0)9 223 62 03
www.souplounge.be

This is a friendly soup bar in a quiet lane overlooking the River Leie. The young cooks in the open kitchen make four different soups in huge simmering pots and serve them in big bowls with bread and an apple. The options range from exotic Thai recipes to a simple tomato soup with meatballs. You can add parsley or croutons from the bowls sitting on the counter. The best tables are upstairs where you can perch at a table with a view of the river.

50 RICHELIEU

Koningin
Astridlaan 210
Station Quarter ⑦
+32 (0)9 222 33 33
richelieugent.be

We think this small delicatessen near the main station makes the best sandwiches in Ghent. The couple who run the shop have come up with a long list of original sandwiches, like the *Broodje Océan*, a delicious combination of herring in sour cream sauce, smoked salmon, sun-dried tomatoes and salad.

The 5 best places for
LUNCH

---

51 CAFÉ RENÉ

Gebroeders
Vandeveldestraat 2
Central Ghent ①
+32 (0)9 223 27 00

This is a lively corner bar with bare brick walls, solid wooden tables and lamps by the British designer Tom Dixon. The kitchen produces plain Belgian cooking at affordable prices, which makes it popular with students, creative professionals and young parents. The dishes are served with a tasty salad, a portion of frites and a pot of mayonnaise. Open from early morning.

52 LEPELBLAD

Onderbergen 40
Central Ghent ①
+32 (0)9 324 02 44
www.lepelblad.be

This relaxed restaurant occupies a 19th-century house with a sober modern interior. It attracts a young, fashionable crowd who come for the friendly service and the buzzing atmosphere. The menu includes fish dishes, tajines, salads and a delicious cheesecake. It's always crowded so you really have to book.

53 PATIRON

Sluizeken 30
Patershol ②
+32 (0)9 233 45 87
www.patiron.be

Here is a friendly lunch spot where they serve delicious quiches and generous salads. The eating area is limited to a few wooden tables at the back of a shop and a little garden in the summer. It looks simple, but the cooking is very good.

54 MUB'ART

Fernand Scribedreef 1
Citadelpark ⑤
+32 (0)9 221 44 89
www.mubart.be

The Museum of Fine Arts has a friendly basement brasserie where you can eat a relatively cheap lunch after a morning looking at Flemish Masters. The interior is designed in a relaxed modern style, while the terrace is a shady spot to eat out in the summer. The kitchen offers simple food like homemade soup, steaks or quiche, along with a few seasonal specialities.

55 DU PROGRÈS

Korenmarkt 10
Central Ghent ①
+32 (0)9 225 17 16
www.duprogres.be

This is a classic Flemish brasserie that has been run by the same family for three generations. The interior is decorated with wood-panelling, brown leather banquettes and rows of mirrors. The waiters are friendly and efficient, while the food is just as you would want in a brasserie. Order steak, frites and a carafe of red wine for a perfect lunch.

54 MUB'ART

The 5 best
BAKERIES AND CAKE SHOPS

---

56 **JULIE'S HOUSE**
Kraanlei 13
Central Ghent ①
+32 (0)9 233 33 90
www.julieshouse.be

Look out for the window filled with pink cupcakes. That's Julie Stampaert's little shop where she sells her sensational cakes, tarts and other sweet things. The shop occupies a restored 19th-century house on the waterfront. It feels like a dolls' house inside, with just a few small tables where you can sample Julie's brunch or try one of her cakes.

57 **JOOST ARIJS**
Vlaanderenstraat 24
Central Ghent ①
+32 (0)9 336 23 10
www.joostarijs.be

The young pastry chef Joost Arijs recently opened a pâtisserie among the Flemish foodie restaurants on Vlaan-derenstraat. The interior is a stylish minimalist design with a long white counter. Here he sells unique cakes, chocolates and macaroons that are like miniature works of art. The 2013 French Gault&Millau food guide listed him as their pastry chef of the year.

58 HIMSCHOOT

Groentenmarkt 1
Central Ghent ①
+32 (0)9 382 66 26
bakkerijhimschoot.be

Here is the perfect place to pick up a currant bun or croissant fresh from the oven. The bakers still work through the night in the cramped basement of this old shop founded in 1906. They bake 65 different types of loaves in four small ovens, including a dense rye bread and a delicious currant bread. The queues can be long, but no one minds the wait when the bread is so much better than anywhere else.

59 JACQUES & PATRICK DUTILLEUL

Goudstraat 31
St-Jacobs Quarter ④
+32 (0)9 225 43 00

This tiny shop near the Vrijdagmarkt is one of the last authentic bakers left in Ghent. They sell the crispest French baguettes and the flakiest croissants, as well as a local speciality known as *mattetaartje*. You may have a long wait on a Sunday morning.

60 MAX

Goudenleeuwplein 3
Central Ghent ①
+32 (0)9 223 97 31
etablissementmax.be

This gorgeous restaurant claims to be the birthplace of the Brussels waffle. Take your children here to eat amid gaudy painted panels salvaged from fairground waffle stands and old photographs of Max Consael, who claims to have invented the fluffy Brussels waffle in 1839 using an iron to press the dough into 20 small squares. The waffles are still made using ancient waffle irons and topped with a light dusting of powdered sugar that covers your clothes as soon as you take the first bite.

The 5 best places for
BRUNCH

---

61 FIN DE FAIM
Hoogstraat 73
Central Ghent ①
+32 (0)9 225 10 25

Diana Terryn has turned a former baker's shop on a busy street into a little Parisian café. She has kept the old Belgian tiled floor and elegant Art Nouveau wooden doors, but painted the walls deep red and added round marble tables and a playlist of French chansons.

62 PAIN PERDU
Walpoortstraat 9
University Quarter ⑥
+32 (0)9 224 18 25
www.painperdugent.be

This is a friendly coffee house with rustic wooden floorboards and a long communal table. Open from eight in the morning, they serve fresh local food, including tasty breads, flaky croissants and pots of delicious home-made Callas jams. The secret garden at the back is one of the most romantic spots we know in Ghent.

63 DEN HOEK AF
Vlaanderenstraat 1
Central Ghent ①

Tom Coone created this relaxed coffee bar using old stuff he picked up in secondhand stores. The counter is decorated with 300 hand-painted wooden slats while the lamps were salvaged from a junk shop. The soup is served in big bowls and the coffee is a mellow variety from a little local supplier called Viva Sara.

64 BARISTA ZUIVELBRUG

Meerseniersstraat 16
Patershol ②
+32 (0)470 52 36 51
www.mybarista.be

This relaxed coffee shop occupies the ground floor of an old stone house that was until recently a flour mill. The white walls are decorated with 105 little drawings by Emilio Lopez-Menchero based on works by Flemish artists of the Latem School. The little terrace in the cobbled lane outside has a few metal tables that sometimes catch the afternoon sun.

65 BROODERIE

Jan Breydelstraat 8
Central Ghent ①
+32 (0)9 225 06 23
www.brooderie.be

This sober café is located in a 17th-century brick building with a step gable roof. The interior is furnished with wooden tables, shelves lined with books and a stack of daily newspapers. It's a popular place for brunch, so arrive early if you want to enjoy the smoked salmon, boiled eggs and Lavazza coffee.

62 PAIN PERDU

The 5 best places for
LATE NIGHT FOOD

66 **MARTINO**
Vlaanderenstraat 125
Central Ghent ①
+32 (0)9 225 01 04

Students are deeply fond of this late-night snack bar where you can pick up a steak and frites or an omelette with a glass of wine when everywhere else is closed. The interior was recently redecorated in a sober modern style, but the big photographs on the wall show how it used to look. An authentic Ghent institution open from 6 pm until 1 am.

67 **DE ROBOT**
Bijlokehof 1
Bijloke Quarter ③
+32 (0)9 335 60 14
www.derobot.be

This is a relaxed café on a corner opposite the old Bijloke hospital. The blue formica tables, tiled floor and potted plants give it a retro look, while the collection of toy robots adds a quirky touch. Students and teachers come here from the art school across the road to eat plain food like hamburgers and lasagne while mellow 1950s music plays in the background. Open most nights until 1 am.

67 DE ROBOT

68 **AU BOEUF QUI RIT**
    Steendam 13
    St-Jacobs Quarter ④
    +32 (0)9 233 72 27

Marianne runs a simple French-style bistro crammed with old family photographs, mirrors and umbrellas. Edith Piaf plays in the background as the owner cooks steaks and lamb chops on a wood fire. She serves them with plain baked potatoes and a salad. It's not sophisticated cooking, yet still you might fall in love with the relaxed French charm. Open until 2 am.

69 CAFÉ GOMEZ

Oude Beestenmarkt 4
St-Jacobs Quarter ④
+32 (0)9 391 22 77
www.cafegomez.be

This new late-night café serves beer and good food to the young party crowd on the Oude Beestenmarkt. The name comes from the former Portuguese striker Nuno Gomes, while the striking ceiling fresco – inspired by Russian prison tattoos – was created by the Ghent graphic artist Benjamin Van Oost. A good spot for a cocktail in the early evening or a midnight snack if you have been out on the town. Open until 3am on Friday and Saturday.

70 GÖK II

Sleepstraat 65
Patershol ②
+32 (0)9 223 38 98
www.gok2.be

The Gök family runs three restaurants in the Turkish quarter named Gök, Gök II and Gök Palace. You might have thought that Gök Palace would be the grand one, but Gök II is more palatial. It occupies a 19th-century town house with lofty moulded ceilings, wood-panelled walls and a little garden for summer evenings. The menu comes with photographs of the dishes so you know exactly what to expect. You can order typical Turkish dishes like grilled meat, moussaka or Turkish pizza. The food is not too bad, but people mainly come here for the friendly staff, the lively atmosphere and the cheap prices. Open until midnight.

The 5 best shops for
BELGIAN CHOCOLATES

---

71 HILDE DEVOLDER
Burgstraat 43
Patershol ②
+32 (0)9 269 02 00

Hilde Devolder creates handmade chocolates in a workshop at the back of her shop. They are sold in little cellophane bags or neat boxes of eight. Devolder also sells chocolate bars by Rózsavölgyi Csokoládé of Hungary and other exclusive brands. And, as Valentine's Day approaches, she displays red chocolate hearts in bowls filled with pink feathers. We love this place.

72 VAN HECKE
Koestraat 42
Central Ghent ①
+32 (0)9 225 43 57
chocolaterievanhecke.be

This little chocolate shop has been run by the same family since 1937. The current owner Stephen Van Hecke supplied Nicole Kidman and her film crew with several boxes of pralines in 2012 while she was filming Grace of Monaco in a building just around the corner.

73 VAN LERBERGE
Kortrijkse-
steenweg 643
Citadelpark ⑤
+32 (0)9 221 87 71
www.vanlerberge.be

This old-fashioned Belgian chocolatier has been selling delicious handmade chocolates since 1953. It is popular with older Ghent people who live in the elegant southern quarter. Try their filled chocolate pralines in the shape of horses' heads.

74 LUC VAN HOOREBEKE

Sint-Baafsplein 15
Central Ghent ①
+32 (0)9 221 03 81
www.chocolatesvan
hoorebeke.be

The Van Hoorebeke family sells hand-made chocolates in a handsome 19th-century shop interior near the Cathedral. Luc Van Hoorebeke founded the business in 1982 and now works alongside his son Cédric, who recently opened his own shop in Jan Breydelstraat. A glass panel in the floor reveals the tiny basement workshop where father and son create some sublime chocolates.

75 YUZU

Walpoortstraat 11a
University Quarter ⑥
+32 (0)473 96 57 33

Nicolas Vanaise finds inspiration for his home-made chocolates during trips to Japan. He creates exquisite chocolates every morning using subtle flavours like fresh yuzu fruit imported from Japan and sometimes goes even further by adding a dash of something local like Ganda ham, Roomer or even spicy Tierentyn mustard.

74 LUC VAN HOOREBEKE

The 5 best places for
AUTHENTIC BELGIAN FRITES

---

76 'T BLAUW KOTJE
Kortrijkse-
steenweg 681
Station Quarter ⑦
+32 (0)9 221 79 73

This snack bar with blue walls and blue furniture lies in the southern suburbs on the route of tram 4. It's a long way from the centre of town, but people drop by because the owners are friendly and the frites are exceptional.

77 MARCEL
Ter Platen 4
University Quarter ⑥
frituurmarcel.be

This is an outstanding frites shop in the university quarter with a stark black and white interior. The friendly women who serve here know how to make the perfect frites. On summer days you can sit outside on the roof terrace or eat your frites at an empty bench down by the waterfront. Closed at weekends.

78 DE GOUDEN SATÉ

Sint-Pietersplein
University Quarter ⑥

This friendly little shop in the university quarter serves delicious frites along with various sauces and meat snacks. On warm days you can sit on a stone bench in the little square opposite while cyclists rush past from every direction. Open through the night until 7 am.

79 DE PAPEGAAI

Annonciadenstraat 17
Central Ghent ①
+32 (0)9 329 00 81

They take time to prepare the frites at De Papegaai (The Parrot). You place your order and then wait for them to be done. It is a rather basic place with hard seats, a TV tuned to a Belgian music channel and faded posters of parrots. But the frites, when they arrive, are exceptional. The smallest portion is more than enough for two.

80 FRIETKETEL

Papegaaistraat 89
Central Ghent ①
+32 (0)9 329 40 22

This is a hugely popular frites shop where they use vegetable oil rather than animal fat. They cut the potatoes by hand every day and fry them twice to create healthy, authentic frites. Students flock here from the nearby college to order a portion of frites topped with a scoop of homemade *stoverij* (a sauce made from thick meaty stew), or a spicy mayonnaise called *samurai*.

The 5 best
FOOD SHOPS

---

81 TIERENTEYN-VERLENT

Groentenmarkt 3
Central Ghent ①
+32 (0)9 225 83 36
www.tierenteyn-verlent.be

This beautiful wood-panelled shop has been selling spicy mustard since 1862. The business was founded even earlier – one year after the French Revolution – by a woman named Adelaide Verlent who had picked up the art of grinding mustard seeds in the Dijon manner. The mustard is made in big wooden vats using a secret recipe and poured into grey stoneware jars decorated with the family signature. It is only sold in this one shop in Ghent.

82 HET HINKELSPEL

Ferdinand Lousbergskaai 33
Dampoort ⑧
+32 (0)9 224 20 96
www.hethinkelspel.be

Three local students started out some years ago making organic cheese in an old Ghent convent. They moved the production out of the city in 2011, but the shop in the heart of the university quarter has survived. They sell three cheeses made with unpasteurised milk, including a unique variety named Dulses flavoured with red algae from the coast of Brittany.

83 VISHANDEL DE VIS

Voldersstraat 48
Central Ghent ①
+32 (0)9 224 32 28
www.devis.be

Danny Decroos drives to the coast every morning to buy cod fresh from the North Sea. But he doesn't stop there. He sometimes flies off to Iceland to find the best halibut, or visits the ports of Denmark to track down the most succulent *maatjes* (raw herring). He has written books on fish cooking and his shop is regularly voted one of the best in Belgium.

84 HUIS DIEGENANT

Sint-Lievenspoort-
straat 228
University Quarter ⑥
+32 (0)9 225 82 94
www.diegenant.be

The Diegenant family has been selling poultry and game since 1878. Their shop has barely changed since 1955 when they installed yellow tiles and a marble counter. They sell the very best Belgian free-range chickens, along with *Poulet de Bresse* and game from the Ardennes.

85 SPICE BAZAAR

Burgstraat 25
Central Ghent ①
+32 (0)9 234 19 15
www.spicebazaar.be

This specialised shop sells exotic spices in long test tubes with cork stoppers. You can find almost any spice you need to cook an Indian curry or a Thai soup. They also stock spices to flavour gin, dried fruits, herbal teas and a set of basic spices for students, along with a small range of edible insects.

The 5 best shops for
BEER AND WINE

---

86 DE HOPDUVEL

Coupure Links 625
Bijloke Quarter ③
+32 (0)9 225 20 68
www.dehopduvel.be

This outstanding beer shop opened in 1982 in a former factory on the Coupure canal. It stocks a huge range of bottles from small breweries around the world. You can pick up elusive beers with odd names like Alive & Kicking, Wijsbier Smoking Gun and Holy Cow! Beer tastings are organised in the shop every Saturday.

87 L'APERO D'OC

Ajuinlei 22
Central Ghent ①
+32 (0)472 53 53 23
www.laperodoc.be

This is a bright modern wine bar on the Leie waterfront where you can pick up wines from the Languedoc-Roussillon region. The owner Eva Tiétard also imports olives, salamis and cheeses from the South-West of France.

88 EVÍN

Sint-Margrietstraat 16
Patershol ②
+32 (0)9 278 54 01
www.evingent.be

This inspiring little wine shop and bar has some rare wines in stock. The owner regularly comes up with creative ideas to sell wine, like after work tastings, DJ concerts and packs of three wines with drinking notes.

89 VINTAGE

Onderbergen 35
Central Ghent ①
+32 (0)9 223 51 32
www.vintage.be

Here is a wine bar where they like to do things differently. It is furnished with small tables, dark wood walls and wooden wine racks. You can taste the wines by the glass or order a whole crate to take home. Vintage has creative chefs in the kitchen who produce interesting three-course menus with wines included.

90 HET WIJNHUIS

Joremaaie 1
Dampoort ⑧
+32 (0)9 223 33 73
www.hetwijnhuis.be

This is a serious wine shop with a sober modern interior in the Portus Ganda quarter. The owner stocks more than 850 different wines from selected vineyards across the world. You can pick up a Riesling from Heribert Boch's vineyard, or a fresh Pinhal da Torre made in the hills to the north of Lisbon.

88 EVÍN

The 5 best
COFFEE ROASTING SHOPS

91 MOKABON

Donkersteeg 35
Central Ghent ⓘ
+32 (0)9 225 71 95
www.mokabon.be

A young Italian immigrant set up this coffee roasting shop in 1937. Hidden down a narrow lane, it is a warm, dark place with old furniture and red neon signs. It attracts women with lapdogs, local students and creative types, as well as tourists who happen to stray down the lane. You can also pick up a takeaway coffee at the counter next door.

92 SAO PAULO

Koestraat 24
Central Ghent ⓘ
+32 (0)9 225 44 11
www.saopaulo.be

The smell of fresh coffee hits you the moment you enter Sao Paulo. They have been roasting coffee here since the Ghent World Fair in 1913. The coffee is stored in a row of gleaming brass dispensers behind the counter. The shop also stocks 200 different types of tea.

93 VANDEKERCKHOVE'S KOFFIEHANDEL

Brabantdam 15
Central Ghent ⓘ
+32 (0)9 225 81 89
www.vdkkoffie.be

Louis Vandekerckhove's family has been involved in the coffee business since 1854. The roasting is done in the basement of the shop using beans shipped from Brazil and Kenya. They sell about 30 different varieties including several unique blends.

94 JAVANA

Hoornstraat 7
Central Ghent ①
+32 (0)9 336 86 46
www.javana.be

Javana is an old Bruges firm that has been roasting coffee since 1949. They opened a branch in Ghent in 2011 in a former cheese shop with a handsome wooden façade. The roast coffee is stored in shiny dispensers, while teas are stored in little wooden drawers.

95 DRAAK

Goudenleeuwplein 1
Central Ghent ①
+32 (0)9 233 02 05
www.dedraak.be

This coffee roasting company was founded in 1864 on the site of a monastery. It sells coffee in an old building in the city centre, along with teas by Dammann Frères, Jura espresso machines and jams by Callas Confiture of Ghent.

91 MOKABON

The 5 local specialities
YOU MUST EAT
IN GHENT

---

96 MASTELLEN
FOUND AT:

Mastelle&Co
Jan Breydelstraat 32
Central Ghent ①
+32 (0)473 71 65 50

This is an old Ghent speciality traditionally eaten during festivals. It consists of a light bun cut in half and spread with cinnamon, butter and brown sugar. The two halves are then covered in aluminium foil and flattened with an iron. You can eat them at a street food stand called Mastelle&Co run by the friendly former boat tour guide Younes Benzaza.

97 RODE NEUZEN
FOUND AT:

Groentenmarkt
Central Ghent ①

These strange soft red sweets shaped like noses are based on an old recipe dating from 1873. Sometimes called Cuberdons, they consist of a hard outer shell enclosing a dark, drippy raspberry syrup. They are sold at two wooden carts near the Gravensteen. Each one claims to be the best, but it is hard to see any difference.

98 GENTSE WATERZOOI

SERVED AT:

Georges IV
Donkersteeg 23
Central Ghent ①
+32 (0)9 225 19 18
www.georges4.be

This is an old Ghent fish stew originally made with river fish caught in the Leie and the Scheldt. But it can also be done using stewing chicken. Every chef has a different recipe, but the basic idea is to cut up potatoes, celery, carrot and leek and simmer with fish or chicken in a creamy broth.

99 GENTSE STOVERIJ

SERVED AT:

Belfort Restaurant
Emile Braunplein 40
Central Ghent ①
+32 (0)9 223 35 65
www.belfort-
restaurant.be

This rich dark stew is made with beef cooked in dark Flemish beer and flavoured with Tierenteyn mustard. Served with frites, it is the perfect dish for a winter day. The Belfort Restaurant in the city centre makes its stoverij using organic meat and dark Leffe beer.

100 ROOMER

FOUND AT:

Hot Club de Gand
Groentenmarkt 15
Central Ghent ①
+32 (0)478 25 67 62
www.hotclubdegand.be

A unique Ghent aperitif sold in distinctive bottles with round bases. It was invented some few years ago by the brothers Maarten and Jeroen Roomer using an old recipe for elderflower wine passed down by their grandmother.

65 PLACES
FOR A DRINK

The 5 most
WELCOMING HIPSTER
COFFEE BARS

---

101 LE JARDIN BOHÉMIEN

Burgstraat 19
Patershol ②
+32 (0)9 328 39 48
lejardinbohemien.be

Young Ghent creatives love this café created by interior designer Jeanpierre De Taeye and sculptor Kristine Dehond where most of the furniture is for sale. It looks like an art studio with its big workshop table, vintage chairs and magazine rack made from old tennis rackets. This is a relaxed place to go for brunch, a slice of tart or a coffee.

102 CLOUDS IN MY COFFEE

Dendermondse-
steenweg 104
Dampoort ⑧
+32 (0)9 336 84 34

Veva van Sloun opened this cool coffee bar in 2012. The Dutch designer Maurice Mentjens created the relaxed interior with bare brick walls, mat black tables and old school chairs. It is located next to a co-housing project in a neighbourhood of Turkish bakeries and cheap clothing stores.

103 OR

Walpoortstraat 26
University Quarter ⑥
+32 (0)9 223 65 00
www.orcoffee.be

A relaxed coffee bar with friendly young baristas trained in the art of coffee making. The coffee is made with beans roasted by a small Flemish company founded in 2001. Students and creative people love this place.

104 GUST

Annonciadenstraat 4
Central Ghent ①
+32 (0)474 41 65 95
www.gustgent.be

A perfect little cafe with designer lamps, round wooden tables and mellow background music. The friendly owner serves American pancakes for brunch, homemade food at lunchtime and really good coffee in delicate china cups.

105 LABATH

Oude Houtlei 1
Central Ghent ①
+32 (0)9 225 28 25
www.cafelabath.be

Students from the Sint-Lucas art academy fill this bright, buzzing coffee bar on weekday mornings. It is a relaxed place with big windows, white wooden chairs and lazy background jazz. The cakes they serve here come from Julie's House.

102 CLOUDS IN MY COFFEE

101 LE JARDIN BOHÉMIEN

The 5 most
STRIKING CAFÉ INTERIORS

---

106 VOORUIT

Sint-Pieters-
nieuwstraat 23
University Quarter ⑥
+32 (0)9 267 28 48
vooruit.be

This grand café occupies the ground floor of a 1913 building created by the socialist organisation Vooruit. It is a beautiful space with marble tables, tiled floors and high ceilings. On sunny days, you can sit outside on a roof terrace added to the side of the building in 2013 by DIAL architects. The friendly young staff take your order at the bar.

107 GRUUT STADSBROUWERIJ

Grote Huidevetters-
hoek 10
University Quarter ⑥
+32 (0)9 269 02 69
+32 (0)472 38 51 48
www.gruut.be

Annick De Splenter opened this impressive brewery in 2009 in a former grain mill on a bend in the River Leie. The interior has a rugged industrial look with a cobbled floor, shiny new brewing kettles and a water channel running through the building. The brewery produces five different beers including the sublime Gruut Blond. Look carefully at the beer mats and you might notice that they conceal secret erotic drawings.

108 STAM CAFE

Godshuizenlaan 2
Bijloke Quarter ③
+32 (0)9 285 83 50
www.stamgent.be

The Ghent city museum has a stunning modern café with glass walls rising out of the water. The minimalist interior design features a black marble floor, white tables and red and grey chairs. It is hard to imagine a more stylish spot to drink an espresso coffee or eat lunch.

109 NTGENT CAFE

Sint-Baafsplein 17
Central Ghent ①
+32 (0)9 225 01 01
www.ntgent.be

Here is a striking modern café located in the lobby of the city theatre NT Gent. Designed in 2013 by the Antwerp firm B-architecten, it has an artistic feel, with black tables, white chairs and gold walls. The curious cartoon figures on the walls are the work of NT Gent's artistic director Wim Opbrouck, who also adds his doodles to the programmes and website.

110 PINK FLAMINGO'S

Onderstraat 55
Central Ghent ①
+32 (0)9 233 47 18
www.pinkflamingos.be

This is a strange café decorated with quirky secondhand stuff from the 1950s. The theme changes every three months depending on the mood of the owner, so it might be Penelope Cruz one time you step inside and a celebration of burlesque next time you pass. There are some odd permanent details amid the clutter, like a naked Barbie chandelier just inside the door and a souvenir Spanish bullfighter on top of an old TV. This place appeals to almost everyone in Ghent from cool musicians to left-wing politicians.

The 5 best bars to
DRINK LIKE A LOCAL

---

111 'T KANON
Meerseniersstraat 17
Central Ghent ①

This is an authentic local café. Maybe too authentic. It is filled with a clutter of old radios, porcelain ornaments and prickly cacti in little pots. The owner is a woman called Nadia who talks in a Ghent accent that is hard to follow if you are not from hereabouts.

112 JAN VAN GENT
Annonciadenstraat 1
Central Ghent ①
+32 (0)9 256 02 03

Here is a brown café with a comfortable old interior furnished with battered sofas, old wooden tables and strange stuffed animal heads. You can drop in at any time of day for an espresso, a Belgian beer or a bowl of soup. The little overgrown garden at the back is the perfect spot to sit on a summer evening with a glass of Keizer Karel beer.

113 ZENON

Sint-Veerleplein 7
Central Ghent ①

Zenon is a friendly local bar next to the old fish market with an owner who has a thing about Greece. The tiled floor and little round marble tables look Belgian. But it's odd to see Greek street signs and car number plates dotted around the place, and odder still if you come here on Greek National Day when the owner throws a big Greek party.

114 DE KARPER

Kortrijksesteenweg 2
Bijloke Quarter ③
+32 (0)495 28 07 07
www.cafedekarper.be

This friendly bar has bare wooden floorboards, a timber counter and beer kegs for tables. It could almost be a saloon bar in the Wild West, except it is filled with Belgian cycling memorabilia, making it a popular place for a late-night beer during the Ghent Six Days race. Football fans also pack in here when Belgium is playing a game.

115 DEN TURK

Botermarkt 3
Central Ghent ①
+32 (0)9 233 01 97
www.cafedenturk.be

Here is the oldest café in Ghent, where music students from the nearby conservatory rub shoulders with local councillors who work in the town hall opposite. The café dates back to 1340, or possibly even 1228, depending on who is telling the story. It is a friendly local place with old photographs on the walls, candles on the tables and jazz playing quietly in the background.

The 5 bars with the
LONGEST BEER LISTS

---

116 HET WATERHUIS AAN DE BIERKANT

Groentenmarkt 9
Central Ghent ①
+32 (0)9 225 06 80
*www.waterhuisaan
debierkant.be*

They take beer seriously in this beautiful bar perched above the River Leie. The interior is filled with tin beer signs, dusty books and hop vines. They offer 16 different beers on tap, including the house beer Gandavum, and a further 150 different bottled brews. The small terrace on the waterfront is the perfect spot for a summer evening if you are lucky enough to find a seat.

117 DULLE GRIET

Vrijdagmarkt 50
St-Jacobs Quarter ④
+32 (0)9 224 24 55
www.dullegriet.be

This old Ghent bar takes its name from a mediaeval cannon on a nearby square. The interior looks as old as the cannon with its heavy wooden stools and beer kegs used as tables. The beer menu lists about 250 brews including the house beer Max, which is served in an expensive long glass supported on a wooden stand. But first there is a little ritual to get out of the way. You have to hand over a shoe which goes into a basket that is then raised to the ceiling. The shoe stays there until you return the empty glass.

118 BROUWZAELE

Ter Platen 17
University Quarter ⑥
+32 (0)9 224 33 92

This is a pleasant family-run bar on the waterfront near Kinepolis with a long list of beers to sample, including Westmalle on tap. The interior is old-fashioned with bare wood floors covered in a dusting of sand.

119 DE TROLLEKELDER

Bij Sint-Jacobs 17
St-Jacobs Quarter ④
+32 (0)9 223 76 96
www.trollekelder.be

An atmospheric bar on three floors with bare brick walls, heavy wood tables and something of a Troll obsession. It's worth trying to get a table by the window for a striking view of the Sint-Jacobskerk across the street. They have eight beers on tap including the elusive Barbar.

120 'T EINDE DER BESCHAVING

Sint-Veerleplein 8
Central Ghent ①

This little local bar near the Gravensteen is decorated with old signs advertising beers that mostly no longer exist. We have no idea why it is called 'The End of Civilisation' because it is a civilised little place. The menu lists more than 60 beers including the fabulous Delirium Tremens.

119 DE TROLLENKELDER

The 5 best bars for
JAZZ AND BLUES

121 MISSY SIPPY

Klein Turkije 16
Central Ghent ①
www.missy-sippy.be

This new hot spot brings blues singers and jazz bands to an ancient building in the heart of Ghent. The owners aim to keep the joint jumping with a busy programme of concerts, DJ sets, dance nights and the occasional poetry reading.

122 HOT CLUB DE GAND

Groentenmarkt 15b
Central Ghent ①
+32 (0)488 02 68 27
www.hotclubdegand.be

It is easy to miss this little jazz club hidden down a dark alley opposite the old meat hall. Founded in 2005, it takes its name from the famous Hot Club de France in Paris. The bar is quiet in the afternoon but turns hot in the evenings when students and music fans squeeze down the narrow passage. The programme features flamenco, folk and blues as well as straight jazz. The little walled courtyard adds to the charm of this place.

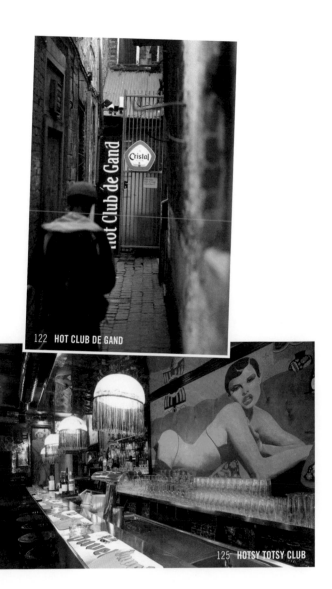

122 HOT CLUB DE GAND

125 HOTSY TOTSY CLUB

123 MINOR SWING

Ottogracht 56
St-Jacobs Quarter ④
+32 (0)494 90 64 83

This small bar with a piano squeezed inside is a popular late night spot. Local actors, musicians and students pile in here to catch a jazz concert or drink one last beer before heading back home. A few tables are put out on the pavement in the summer to catch the afternoon sun.

124 MANTECA

Cataloniëstraat 2
Central Ghent ①

Not many people know about this hidden cocktail bar located in an old building from 1673. The curtains are closed during the day, but someone stirs to open up the place around 4pm. The barman serves very good cocktails that are not too pricey.

125 HOTSY TOTSY CLUB

Hoogstraat 1
Central Ghent ①
+32 (0)9 224 20 12

This classic jazz bar has been around since 1973. Created by Johan and Guido Claus (brothers of the more famous Hugo), it was modelled on Al Capone's Hotsy Totsy Club in Chicago. Initially a private club for artists and writers, this was where Hugo Claus launched his novel The Sorrow of Belgium in 1983. A poem by Claus in praise of the café can be read on an outside wall. The three brothers are all dead now, but this is still a unique jazz club where you can listen to blues or poetry deep into the night.

The 5 most
MELLOW CAFES
& COFFEE BARS

---

126 SIMON SAYS

Sluizeken 8
Patershol ②
+32 (0)9 233 03 43
www.simon-says.be

This is a relaxed coffee bar in a forgotten part of town near the Patershol. It was opened by Simon Turner and Christopher Joseph who also run a small B&B in the same bright red and yellow Art Nouveau building. The tables are covered with hand-made tiles while the dark blue walls are dotted with tiny drawings of imaginary flying machines by the Antwerp artist Panamarenko. The coffee comes from a chunky Faema machine that sits on the counter along with croissants and cakes.

127 GUSTAF

Sint-Jacobs-
nieuwstraat 45
St-Jacobs Quarter ④
+32 (0)472 98 06 53
*www.espressobargustaf.
be*

You may have trouble finding a table in this tiny coffee bar furnished with pale wood tables, black chairs and a single bookshelf. The mood is relaxed, with magazines to read and jazz playing quietly in the background. The owner makes superb coffee using beans from plantations in Sulawesi and Kenya. He also serves delicious chocolate cake made by a friend.

128 HET SALON

Sint-Pieters-
nieuwstraat 194
University Quarter ⑥
+32 (0)9 225 03 55

This spacious light-filled café describes itself as 'your living room since 1982'. That is just about right. It is furnished in a warm 1980s style with pine tables and potted plants. They play cool indie music and offer free jugs of water. You can come here for an early morning breakfast, a quick sandwich at lunchtime or a coffee to see you through the afternoon. The room at the back overlooks a little Zen garden and there is a secret roof terrace to soak up the sun at the top of the stairs.

129 SPHINX

Sint-Michielshelling 3
Central Ghent ①
www.sphinx-cinema.be

This quiet café is attached to the Sphinx arthouse cinema in the city centre. The friendly barman makes a good Illy coffee to grab before a film. Or you can drink a glass of cava while you check your emails using the free wifi. They also keep a couple of chess sets behind the bar to pass away an afternoon.

130 ROMAIN

Walpoortstraat 13
University Quarter ⑥
+32 (0)477 68 05 71

This warm, mellow café was once filled with religious statues, but it is now a shrine to the actor Romain Deconinck. The walls are covered with old theatre posters and photographs from the days when Romain entertained local audiences at the old Minnemeers theatre next door. The yellow metal chairs on the terrace outside get snapped up as soon as the sun comes out.

The 5 best

BARS TO HEAR
NEW BANDS

---

131 DE LOGE

Annonciadenstraat 5
Central Ghent ①
+32 (0)9 225 34 38
www.deloge.be

You might easily walk past this café. It does not look too interesting from the outside, yet De Loge is one of the hidden gems of Ghent. The interior is furnished with tables painted by children, an old piano and a bookcase crammed with paperback novels. You can come here for breakfast, a cheap lunch or just a glass of wine. They have free concerts on Wednesday and Sunday nights, along with the occasional literary event. We love the strange secret salon on the first floor.

132 KINKY STAR BAR

Vlasmarkt 9
St-Jacobs Quarter ④
+32 (0)9 223 48 45
www.kinkystar.com

This alternative music club has been around for more than a decade. It has two stages where almost every band in East Flanders has performed over the years. It also hosts evenings devoted to poetry, comedy and even tap dancing. Kinky Star also runs a radio station and a music academy.

133 DE KLEINE KUNST

Ferdinand
Lousbergskaai 99
University Quarter ⑥
+32 (0)484 03 98 93
cafedekleinekunst.be

This relaxed waterfront bar in the Visserij district has a gentle old-fashioned feel. They play music from the 1970s and organise acoustic concerts twice a week. The beers on tap include Karmeliet Tripel and Grimbergen Blonde. They also serve some simple food such as spaghetti, *hutsepot* (stew) in winter and the local speciality *droge worst* (dry sausage).

134 CAFÉ VIDEO

Oude Beestenmarkt 7
St-Jacobs Quarter ④
cafevideo.be

Look out for the bright green and blue corner house. The band Das Pop used to rehearse in an upstairs room before they became famous. This is a relaxed music bar where upcoming bands perform on the stage most nights. Entry is free and the beer hardly costs more than a couple of euro. But don't talk during the concerts. And put that phone away. People come here to listen to the band.

135 CLUB RESERVA

Jan Breydelstraat 32
Central Ghent ①
+32 (0)498 54 11 17
www.clubreserva.be

This relaxed café was created a few years ago by the owners of the Hot Club de Gand. They have a long list of whiskies and rums, as well as some interesting beers. People drop in during the day for a bowl of soup or a slice of cheesecake. Musicians turn up four nights a week to give free concerts of jazz, classical music or chanson.

The 5 most
ROMANTIC CAFES

---

136 HUSET
Hoogstraat 49
Central Ghent ①
www.husetgent.be

Here is a strange, romantic place hidden away in a vast Ghent mansion. It is run as a café and gallery by Eveline Roels, a Ghent art graduate who grew up in this grand 1860s house. You sit on worn antique chairs under a beautiful moulded ceiling while Eveline heats up some soup in the kitchen or brings you coffee in a delicate China cup. It is a warm, welcoming place with a beautiful overgrown garden at the back for summer days. 'Huset is a place where anything can happen,' Eveline says. But unfortunately not at weekends, when it is closed.

137 HUIZE COLETTE
Belfortstraat 6
Central Ghent ①
+32 (0)478 90 64 73

Two young women called Aline and Ottelien have created a relaxed, bohemian café filled with second-hand books, old lamps and antique framed photographs of young lovers. The coffee comes on a silver tray and the croissants are served with a small pot of jam.

But the speciality of the house is a hot chocolate drink based on a 17th-century English recipe that uses melted chocolate, hot water and spices. It can get crowded downstairs, but you can usually find a table on the first floor.

138 ROCOCO

Corduwaniers-
straat 57
Patershol ②
+32 (0)9 224 30 35

Hidden down a cobbled lane in the Patershol, this is a wonderful place for a late-night drink. It feels like a private home, furnished with assorted tables and chairs, piles of books, candles everywhere and an old piano. Out at the back is an overgrown garden that is deeply poetic on summer evenings. But the main attraction is Betty, who has been in charge of this place for the past 25 years. She mingles with her customers, invites local musicians to play and occasionally offers flirting couples a glass of her secret love potion Elixir d'Amour.

139 DE ALCHEMIST

Rekelingestraat 3
Central Ghent ①
+32 (0)493 55 31 53

This romantic little bar opposite the Gravensteen is the perfect place to dive inside on a wet winter day. The interior has a warm, welcoming feel with its old rococo wood-panelling, candles in gin bottles and stuffed deer head. The beer list includes some interesting Ghent brews, but this is really a place to drink a gin and tonic or possibly, if you are feeling extravagant, a glass of Ben Nevis whisky bottled 42 years ago.

140 DE GEUS VAN GENT

Kantienberg 9
University Quarter ⑥
+32 (0)9 220 78 25
www.geuzenhuis.be

This café is hidden down a quiet cobbled lane that runs beside the Sint-Pietersabdij. You would never come across it by accident. Yet it is one of the most romantic spots in Ghent, especially if you can find a table in the room to the left. Here you are surrounded by bookshelves, oil paintings and curious animal heads. Open from 4 pm until the last customer heads out into the damp Ghent night.

136 **HUSET**

The 5 best terraces for
SITTING IN THE SUN

---

141 DE PLANCK
Ter Platen 10
University Quarter ⑥
+32 (0)478 76 94 16
www.deplanck.be

This is an old river barge where you can sit out under the trees on a warm summer evening. The menu lists 125 beers, including the house brew Planckske. The barge lies moored on the waterfront near Kinepolis cinema, making it a hot spot for movie fans.

142 BARRAZZA
Hoefslagstraatje 6
Central Ghent ①
+32 (0)472 94 53 24
www.barrazza.be

Dieter and Robin run this friendly coffee bar in an old 16th-century house with roses growing up the walls. It lies at the end of a quiet lane overlooking the Leie. The interior has tables looking out on the water and odd vintage details like an old radio and photographs of King Baudouin and Queen Fabiola.

143 BAR JAN CREMER
Kramersplein 5
University Quarter ⑥
+32 (0)474 24 85 93
barjancremer.be

This relaxed bar is named after the notorious Dutch novelist Jan Cremer. The architect Wim Goes has created a cool interior featuring pale wood tables and walls stripped back to the bare brick. It has a huge terrace on the square with bright orange deckchairs and little round tables scattered around in the summer to create the mood of a beach café.

144 HET SPIJKER

Pensmarkt 3
Central Ghent ①
+32 (0)9 329 44 40
www.cafehetspijker.be

This historic bar is located in a rugged grain warehouse with bare brick walls and low beams. Be careful when you enter or you will hit your head on the 12th-century stone lintel. If the weather is at all warm everyone likes to sit out on the terrace at the front, but only a few know about the waterfront spot at the back of the café where you can sit with a Belgian beer looking out on the river.

145 LUNCHCAFE WALRY

Zwijnaardse-
steenweg 6
Citadelpark ⑤
+32 (0)9 220 00 18

Hidden away behind a modern bookshop, this café stands on the site of an old garage. The garden is shaded by old trees, making the perfect spot for a drink on a hot summer day.

145 LUNCHCAFÉ WALRY

The 5 most
UNUSUAL CAFES

---

146 LOKAAL

Brabantdam 100
Central Ghent ①
+32 (0)477 19 95 44

This is a new lunch spot located at the end of a 19th century arcade where prostitutes pose in shop windows. But there is nothing seedy about Lokaal. The bohemian interior is furnished with quirky chairs, vinyl records and pots of herbs. The owners serve tasty vegetable soups and salads made with vegetables grown locally, along with pots of herbal tea.

147 DREUPELKOT

Groentenmarkt 12
Central Ghent ①
+32 (0)9 224 21 20
www.dreupelkot.be

The last genever bar in Ghent lies at the end of a narrow alley. Here is one of the last places in Belgium where you can taste the traditional drink of the Low Countries distilled from a mixture of grain and malt. The owner creates his own versions by adding a dash of orange or vanilla.

148 'T VELOOTJE

Kalversteeg 2
Patershol ②

This bohemian bar occupies an old house hidden down a cobbled lane. It is truly a strange place to stumble upon. The interior is crammed with old newspapers and assorted junk. Several dozen old bicycles hang from the ceiling along with bird cages and religious relics. The beer list is limited and somewhat overpriced, but you come here for the atmosphere. Some people love it. Others worry that a bicycle will fall on their head or they will catch a disease.

149 TEMPUS FUGIT
Koningin Maria
Hendrikaplein
Station Quarter ⑦
+32 (0)9 245 56 18

Tempus Fugit Irreparibile, it says below the big clock in Ghent's main station café. 'Time flies relentlessly onwards,' is the message. More than 100 years have passed since this café opened for the 1913 World Fair. Like almost everything built in Ghent at that time, it looks like a mediaeval banqueting hall, with lofty tiled ceilings, marble columns and neo-gothic wood panelling. You can drink excellent Italian coffee here or a strong Belgian beer.

150 MONTPARNASSE
Bij Sint-Jacobs 9
St-Jacobs Quarter ④

Locals like to drink amid the clutter in this antique shop opposite the Sint-Jacobskerk. The tables are squeezed in among old cupboards, oil paintings and chandeliers. It might seem a strange place to go for a beer, but it has a certain rambling charm. They serve brunch with cava from 7am at the weekend when the antique market is held on the cobbled square outside.

The 5 smartest
COCKTAIL BARS

---

151 JIGGER'S
Oudburg 16
Patershol ②
+32 (0)9 335 70 25
www.jiggers.be

Olivier Jacobs started this cocktail bar with his girlfriend in 2012. Keen to create a sense of mystery, he called it The Noble Drugstore and placed a stuffed fox wearing a monocle in the window. It is a tiny place so you have to phone in advance on the day to book a table. But it is worth all the effort. The bar feels like a private club and the cocktails are magnificent.

152 OLD FASHIONED
Hoogpoort 19
Central Ghent ①
+32 (0)9 279 52 15
www.old-fashioned.be

This mellow cocktail bar is decorated in speakeasy style with low lights and photographs of King Baudouin. Soft jazz whispers from the speakers while bartenders Steve and Tom create unique cocktails based on drinks they have discovered on their travels. Their Apple Pie Martini was inspired by a cocktail they sipped in Amsterdam's Skybar, while The Cuberdon is their own invention. Look out for jazz concerts on Saturdays and absinthe tastings once a month.

153 LIMONADA

Heilige-Geeststraat 7
Central Ghent ①
+32 (0)9 233 78 85

Here is a fun cocktail bar with a striking new interior inspired by the cult science fiction film Tron. It attracts a younger crowd with its quirky cocktails.

154 CAFÉ THEATRE

Schouwburgstraat 5
Central Ghent ①
+32 (0)9 265 05 50
www.cafetheatre.be

This is a stylish cocktail bar on two floors with dark brown chairs and little round tables. It opens in the morning to serve coffee, but mainly exists to shake up exotic cocktails until deep into the night. Don't miss the toilets in the basement, which are decorated in the style of Turkish baths with marble benches, red cushions and tiled basins. Men use the door marked Gazou.

155 VOLTA.BAR

Nieuwe Wandeling 2b
Central Ghent ①
+32 (0)9 324 05 00
www.volta-gent.be

Located in a former turbine hall on the edge of the old town, Volta. is a cool spot to drink a cocktail. The young bartender Erik Veldhuis shakes up some original mixes in the handsome industrial interior. You can also eat in the bar, or book a table in the stylish restaurant down below.

The 5 most inspiring
HYBRID CAFES

---

156 BARBIDON
Bisdomkaai 25
Central Ghent ①
+32 (0)495 24 76 97
www.barbidon.be

The latest trend in Ghent is to open hybrid cafes that offer more than just coffee. Ghent's newest bike shop is one such place. It sells smart city bikes, quirky helmets by Nutcase and fashionable accessories. But it also has a bright modern coffee bar serving Or coffee and croissants.

157 DE WASBAR
Nederkouter 109
Bijloke Quarter ③
+32 (0)485 42 34 32
www.wasbar.be

Here is the coolest place in Belgium to wash your clothes. Yuri and Dries have created a stylish launderette that looks like a 1950s milk bar. You can drink a coffee, order a beer or even get a haircut while your clothes are in the wash. The place is decorated with quirky details like old wooden drawers attached to the walls and T-shirts hung from washing lines. They even have DJ concerts on a Thursday night. But don't try to pay by cash as they only take cards.

158 LE BAR DEPOT

Beverhoutplein 14
St-Jacobs Quarter ④
+32 (0)485 44 04 25

Here is an inspiring place to go for coffee after looking around the flea market. You sit on old armchairs surrounded by antique vases, paintings and chandeliers. Or you can perch at a wobbly table on the cobbled square hoping that the sun will emerge from behind a cloud. The bar opens at 6 am on days when the market is held (Friday to Sunday) serving antique dealers with champagne and croissants.

159 BAR-BIER

Sint-Margrietstraat 18
Patershol ②
+32 (0)9 223 45 93

This appealing little café near the Gravensteen is combined with a hairdresser's salon. You wait downstairs with a coffee and a newspaper, then head upstairs to the salon when it is your turn. The interior is decorated with antique barber's equipment to add to the charm. Open until 10 pm on Thursdays and Fridays, but you will have to book an appointment.

160 COUPE MAISON

Ham 101
Dampoort ⑧
+32 (0)9 278 95 85
www.coupemaison.be

Here is one of the coolest new spots in town, where you can go for a haircut followed by a glass of cava. It's a stylish relaxed place located on the ground floor of a renovated 19th century townhouse. You start by getting your hair done and then sit with a drink and a magazine in the stylish lounge. They are open long hours so you can drop by after work. But you have to book.

The 5 best
LOCAL BEERS
and where to drink them

---

161 GRUUT BLOND

Stadbrouwerij Gruut
Grote Huidevetters-
hoek 10
University Quarter ⑥
+32 (0)9 269 02 69
www.gruut.be

The sublime Gruut Blond is brewed
in an old factory next to the river. It is
flavoured in the mediaeval way using a
mixture of herbs known as Gruut, rather
than the more common hops. The result
is a fresh, light beer with a complex
taste. You can drink Gruut Blond or its
four sister beers in local cafés or straight
from the vats in the brew house down
by the river.

162 GENTSE STROP

Belfort Stadscafé
Emile Braunplein 40
Central Ghent ①
+32 (0)9 225 60 05
www.belfort-stadscafe.be

Gentse Strop is a light fruity beer with
a hint of hops named after the *strop* or
noose that Ghent's leaders were forced
to wear after a failed 16th-century tax
revolt. Brewed near Oudenaarde by the
Roman brewery, it was only launched in
2011, but has already become something
of a cult drink in Ghent.

163 GENTSE TRIPEL

Galgenhuisje
Groentenmarkt 5
Central Ghent ①
+32 (0)9 233 42 51

The Hopduivel beer store commissioned this blond Belgian abbey beer flavoured with hops. The label is decorated with a drawing of the famous three towers of Ghent, although the beer is brewed outside the city at the Steenberge brewery in Ertvelde. It is a strong beer with a complex taste.

164 LOUSBERG

De Walrus
Coupure Links 497
Bijloke Quarter ③
+32 (0)9 279 38 48
www.walrus-gent.be

The people behind Hinkelspel cheese-making cooperative launched this strong, spicy malt beer in 2007. It is produced in limited batches by a small brewery outside Ghent. It is hard to track down, although several bars in Ghent keep a few bottles in the cellar.

165 DELIRIUM TREMENS

Backdoor Café
Sint-Amandstraat 26
University Quarter ⑥

This strong beer was launched in 1989 by an old brewery just outside Ghent. The beer is sold in distinctive ceramic-style bottles decorated with a pink elephant logo. It might seem like a cheeky joke, but this is a serious ale that has been voted best beer in the world.

PIET MOODSHOP

45 PLACES TO SHOP

The 5 best
SMALL AND UNUSUAL SHOPS

---

166 FALLEN ANGELS
Jan Breydelstraat 29
Central Ghent ①
+32 (0)9 223 94 15
the-fallen-angels.com

Isabelle Steel runs this dark, nostalgic shop filled with eccentric objects picked up in strange places. She named it after a batch of abandoned angels she picked up when she opened the shop in 1980. As well as angels, the shop is crammed with tin toys, old school equipment and china dolls with sad glass eyes.

167 VITS-STAELENS
Bij Sint-Jacobs 14
St-Jacobs Quarter ④
+32 (0)9 223 14 69

This is a strange old grocery store on a street corner facing the Sint-Jacobskerk. It is filled with the exotic smell of herbs and spices sold in little cellophane bags. Here you can find everything you need to flavour a vegetarian curry, along with tea, pasta and dried fruits.

168 PRIEM
Zuivelbrugstraat 1
Patershol ②
+32 (0)9 223 25 37

This old wallpaper shop has barely changed since it opened back in 1928. Run by two elderly sisters, it is crammed with more than 10,000 rolls of rare vintage wallpaper dating from the 1950s to the 1980s. They stock every style imaginable, from bold striped wallpaper to vintage floral designs.

169 BURKELBLOEM

Dampoortstraat 92
Dampoort ⑧
+32 (0)9 223 47 37

This crowded little shop on the road leading to Dampoort station is filled with a glorious jumble of old objects. You squeeze between bird cages, faded postcards, decorated tin boxes and gold-rimmed coffee cups salvaged from bankrupt French hotels.

170 BLANCO BIKE LUXURY

Bennesteeg 7
Central Ghent ①
+32 (0)497 62 10 02
blancobikeluxury.be

Thomas Wittouck constructs solid modern bikes in a garage in downtown Ghent. He likes simple bikes that get you across town rather than expensive flashy models. He also does bike repairs and offers useful advice on cycling in Ghent. Open on Fridays and Saturdays only.

168 PRIEM

The 5 best
INDEPENDENT
BOOKSHOPS

---

171 PAARD VAN TROJE
Kouter 113
Central Ghent ①
+32 (0)9 330 08 83
www.paardvantroje.be

This inspiring independent bookshop moved to a new location near the opera house and added a smart coffee bar and pavement terrace. The owner Bart Van Aken worked as a DJ before opening his first bookshop in 2003. He sees no point in stocking beststellers, but instead woos customers inside with unusual and eclectic titles such as the Wood Fire Handbook and Cool Sheds. He also sells a small selection of indie CDs and a few bottles of his favourite wines.

172 LIMERICK
Koningin Elisabeth-
laan 142
Station Quarter ⑦
+32 (0)9 222 17 57
www.limerick.be

Located near the main station, Limerick is a serious literary bookshop with creaking wood floors, comfortable armchairs and the smell of fresh coffee. The owner takes an interest in new fiction in English, French and Dutch, as well as non-fiction books on philosophy and politics. A room at the back contains an odd collection of 160 antique typewriters once owned by the Dutch novelist Willem Frederik Hermans.

171 PAARD VAN TROJE

173 WALRY

174 COPYRIGHT

173 WALRY

Zwijnaardse-
steenweg 6
Citadelpark ⑤
+32 (0)9 222 91 67
www.walry.be

This beautiful literary bookshop attracts students and book lovers with its relaxed mood and striking modern interior by Ghent architect Dirk Defraeye. It specialises in Dutch fiction, history and philosophy, but also maintains a large selection of contemporary Spanish and Italian literature. Literary events are sometimes held in a little café at the end of the garden.

174 COPYRIGHT

Jakobijnenstraat 8
Central Ghent ①
+32 (0)9 223 57 94
copyrightbookshop.be

Hilde Peleman opened this inspiring art bookshop in 1986. It occupies a traditional Ghent town house with three connected rooms and high stucco ceilings. The shelves and tables are stacked with gorgeous books on architecture, contemporary art, design and fashion. Peleman also stocks international art magazines and limited-edition books, as well as hosting the occasional book launch.

175 ATLAS & ZANZIBAR

Kortrijkse-
steenweg 19
Bijloke Quarter ③
+32 (0)9 220 87 99
www.atlaszanzibar.be

This is a serious travel bookshop where you can pick up guide books and maps covering the world's most remote places. The map section is particularly impressive and includes inspiring walking and cycling guides to areas of Belgium that are worth exploring, like the Ypres battlefields, the coast and the Ardennes. You can also buy a useful map showing the extensive cycle network around Ghent.

The 5 best

INDEPENDENT RECORD STORES

176 MUSIC MANIA

Sint-Pieters-
nieuwstraat 19
University Quarter ⑥
+32 (0)477 77 07 43
musicmaniarecords.be

This corner record store near Vooruit has been around since 1969. Local DJs come here to flip through the vinyl LPs in search of elusive finds and exciting new sounds to play to fans. The store also sells record players and music DVDs.

177 VINYL KITCHEN

Lange Violette-
straat 160
University Quarter ⑥
+32 (0)474 25 55 06
www.vinylkitchen.be

This is a relaxed second-hand record store in an old Ghent house with mosaic floors and comfortable armchairs. Music lovers spend hours here hunting through racks of old vinyl records from the 1960s and 1970s. The shop is also visited by local DJs looking for fresh sounds to play on Friday nights.

178 VYNILLA

Sint-Kwintensberg 38
University Quarter ⑥
+32 (0)9 223 71 22
www.vynilla.be

Bob Driege has been selling records in the student quarter for more than 30 years. He stocks an eclectic mix of second-hand vinyl as well as some new releases, and loves nothing more than to talk to his customers about alternative bands, African music and new electronic releases.

179 DUNE RECORDS

Geldmunt 17
Central Ghent ①
+32 (0)9 225 67 84

This store founded in 1993 specialises in obscure music by unknown bands. The owner is proud to tell you that his shop is the only place in the world to sell the LP soundtrack for the 1992 TV series *The Big Battalions*. So now you know.

180 WOOL-E SHOP

Emiel Lossystraat 17
Dampoort ⑧
+32 (0)9 229 36 67
www.wool-e-shop.be

This music store in the eastern suburbs is filled with crates of LPs, old CDs and concert posters. The owner is fond of dark 1980s genres like Punk, Gothic and Deathrock. He often closes early to get to a concert in Antwerp or Kortrijk, so best to check his blog or Facebook page before making the trip out of town.

178 VYNILLA

The 5 best
DESIGN STORES

---

181 PIET MOODSHOP

Sint-Pieters-
nieuwstraat 94
University Quarter ⑥
+32 (0)9 278 69 78
www.pietmoodshop.be

Christophe Verbeke started out with a pop-up store selling inspiring design and fashion. He now has a permanent shop in an old interior with a beautiful tiled floor. Verbeke's carefully-curated selection includes beautiful objects by Martin Margiela and Tom Dixon, as well as a small flower shop at the back. The old shop interior adds to the charm of this place.

182 HUMØR BY REWIND

Bennesteeg 19
Central Ghent ①
+32 (0)9 328 04 87
www.rewindstore.be

The people behind Rewind (two beautiful fashion boutiques for women and men in the Sint-Pietersnieuwstraat) created this smart design store hidden down a quiet back street. Here they sell products by Scandinavian brands like Hay and Samsøe & Samsøe to brighten up city apartments. They also sell bright scarves by Ghent designer Roos Vandekerckhove, along with dresses, jewellery and notebooks.

183 HUISZWALUW

Hoogpoort 3b
Central Ghent ①
+32 (0)9 233 27 37
www.huiszwaluw.com

A beautiful interior design shop with bare wood floors, whitewashed brick walls and vases filled with flowers. The owner has a passion for affordable Scandinavian design, including modern wallpaper by Missprint and Lightyear lamps.

184 YDEE

Oudburg 56
Patershol ②
+32 (0)9 395 00 44
www.ydee.be

Here is an inspiring design shop filled with original furniture, linen and household equipment. The owner has an eye for uncommon European designers like Hay of Denmark and Billiani of Italy.

185 SURPLUS

Zwartezusterstraat 9
Central Ghent ①
+32 (0)9 223 52 94
www.surplusinterieur.be

This cool white store has been selling contemporary design for more than 25 years. They stock a mixture of styles including striking chairs by Carl Hansen and quirky lamps by Established & Sons.

181 PIET MOODSHOP

The 5 best shops for
UNUSUAL GIFTS

---

186 A.PUUR.A

Onderbergen 56
Central Ghent ①
+32 (0)9 223 02 41
apuura.com

Katrien Buyle has been selling beautiful handcrafted objects in her Ghent shop since 1998. She stocks hand-made boxes, leather bags and cashmere coats, as well as unique notebooks and photo albums.

187 A'PRIL

Burgstraat 27
Patershol ②
+32 (0)9 223 09 92

Here is an inspiring gift shop in a beautiful 19th-century interior. It is crammed with odd Japanese notebooks, colourful toasters, eccentric tea pots and quirky birthday cards. This is the place to hunt for a little gift for a niece or a housewarming present for a friend.

188 ZSA-ZSA ROUGE

Serpentstraat 22
Central Ghent ①
+32 (0)9 225 93 63
www.zsazsarouge.be

Located down a quiet cobbled lane, this quirky gift shop is run by the same people as Pink Flamingo's bar, so don't expect anything too serious. The interior is crammed with brightly-coloured kitchen equipment, retro dresses and kitsch objects that no one really needs.

189 AXESWAR DESIGN

Sint-Pieters-
nieuwstraat 12
University Quarter ⑥
+32 (0)9 233 42 43
www.axeswardesign.be

The owners of this bright little shop sell vintage furniture they pick up at design fairs, along with bizarre gadgets from all over. There is nowhere better in Belgium to hunt for garden gnomes, retro coasters or a box of emergency moustaches.

190 MUSEUMSHOP HUIS VAN ALIJN

Kraanlei 67
Central Ghent ①
+32 (0)9 269 23 50
www.huisvanalijn.be

The Huis van Alijn has a beautiful little shop on the waterfront with a wooden front and a bell that rings loudly when you enter. It sells old-fashioned toys and nostalgic games, as well as a series of postcards showing Belgians setting off on family holidays in the 1960s in their shiny new cars.

188 ZSA-ZSA ROUGE

The 5 best
ANTIQUE SHOPS

---

191 HET TIJDREISBUREAU

Ottogracht 35
St-Jacobs Quarter ④
+32 (0)496 55 96 81
www.tijdreisbureau.be

The Ghent designers Fred + Eric recently came up with the slightly mad idea of turning an antique shop into a time travel agency. The windows are covered with special offers on flights to the past, business cards are made to look like airline luggage tags and a curious time machine sits in the middle of the shop. The genial owner Michel Frommer stocks unexpected finds, including 1950s furniture, toy cars and rare vinyl records. He also rents out vintage props to movie companies in need of a stuffed horse or suit of armour.

192 ANTIEK-DEPOT

Baudelostraat 15
St-Jacobs Quarter ④
+32 (0)477 60 61 99
www.antiek-depot.com

Here is a vast antique store located in a former 1902 ironworks. It is occupied by 15 different dealers who have separate collections spread over two floors. You can find anything you want here, including cinema seats, Danish designer chairs, children's toys and doors salvaged from old houses.

191. HET TIJDREISBUREAU

193 MENEERTJE ANTIEK

Baudelostraat 5
St-Jacobs Quarter ④
+32 (0)489 69 48 29

Stijn Brouns and Peter Antheunis opened this offbeat antique shop in 2012. They sell old radios, comic books and biscuit tins, along with a few bottles of fine wine.

194 HET ARCHIEF

Steendam 110
St-Jacobs Quarter ④
+32 (0)9 223 52 00
www.het-archief.be

Hannelore Stassijns runs an appealing shop filled with curiosities. You find old board games, wall maps from Belgian schoolrooms and vintage posters. We admire her loving affection for old things.

195 DEPOT09

Nieuwevaart 118
Northern Ghent
www.depot09.be

Depot09 is a huge industrial space in Ghent docklands where 15 Belgian and Dutch dealers display vintage furniture, lights and design objects. You can track down enamel signs, 1950s tables and quirky objects to add a touch of humour to a loft interior. Or you can buy a gigantic piece of old machinery. The warehouse is easily reached by car if you decide to pick up something you have spotted on their website.

The 5 most romantic
FLOWER SHOPS

196 **ROZEN DOEN BLOZEN**
Wijzemanstraat 6
St-Jacobs Quarter ④
+32 (0)9 279 39 92

Anne-Catherine Platel sells roses in a romantic shop with a pale blue front near the Sint-Jacobskerk. She stocks varieties with wistful poetic names, like Upper Secret and Deep Water, which she uses to create gorgeous bouquets.

197 **NICK BOUSSE**
Sint-Niklaasstraat 10
Central Ghent ①
+32 (0)9 233 22 33
www.nickbousse.be

Nick Bousse opened a little flower shop in Ghent after qualifying as a master florist in the Netherlands. He creates inspiring bouquets using hand-picked flowers combined with unexpected details.

198 **VOLCKAERT**
Vrijdagmarkt 45
St-Jacobs Quarter ④
+32 (0)9 223 23 35
www.bloemen-
volckaert.be

This friendly flower shop has been around since 1973. The owners sell plants for balconies and beautiful bouquets that make perfect gifts if you have been invited to dinner.

199 **BOS BLOEMEN**

Vlaanderenstraat 64
Central Ghent ①
+32 (0)491 50 15 56

The fashion designer Eva Bos recently opened a flower shop next to her boutique. She sells tulips, roses and orchids in a sensual Art Deco interior. Many of her customers are young women looking for something special to hold on their wedding day.

200 **VERVAECKE**

Sint-Jacobs-
nieuwstraat 32
St-Jacobs Quarter ④
+32 (0)9 234 29 60
www.vervaecke-wim.be

Wim Vervaecke has worked in Ghent as a florist for the past 30 years. His shop is filled with stunning orchids in white pots and cut flowers in tall vases. A qualified master florist, he creates sensual bouquets for weddings and special events.

The 5 most beautiful
SHOP INTERIORS

---

201 TÉLESCO SHOP

Groentenmarkt 14
Central Ghent ①
+32 (0)9 225 20 56
telescoshop.be

Télesco occupies an Art Deco shop interior that has hardly changed since it opened in 1939. Located opposite the old meat hall, the family-run shop has a polished wooden floor, dark wood panelling and ornate lamps. Télesco started out selling umbrellas, but recently expanded its stock to include hats, gloves and bags.

202 APOTHEEK VOORUIT DE STEUR

Sint-Pietersplein 26
University Quarter ⑥

This traditional pharmacy is located in a beautiful Art Deco shop dating from 1923. Founded by the Vooruit cooperative, it still has its original stained glass windows as well as wooden shelves lined with old porcelain jars.

203 TIMMERMANS 1845

Kortemunt 5
Central Ghent ①
+32 (0)9 223 32 57
timmermans1845.be

Located in a beautiful baroque building facing the Groentenmarkt, Timmermans has been in business since 1845. The interior has been modernised, but it still has a long wooden counter and rows of little drawers with intriguing handwritten labels. The shop sells pens, Moleskine notebooks and handbags.

204 DE BANIER

Hoefslagstraatje 1
Central Ghent ①
+32 (0)9 233 87 87
www.debanier.be

You may not need a ball of twine or a face-painting kit, but you should still take a look inside this craft shop run by the Flemish Chiro movement. It occupies a beautiful 18th-century waterfront house hidden down a narrow lane. The building still has a row of six cashier counters dating from the time when it was occupied by a stockbroker's firm.

205 AU BON MARCHÉ

Hoornstraat 4
Central Ghent ①
+32 (0)9 269 02 60

Caroline Verheugen sells beautiful leather bags and quirky hats in an old pharmacist's shop with a tiled floor and wooden shelves. She also stocks unique jewellery by Wouters & Hendrix of Antwerp. But nothing is cheap here despite the shop name.

202 APOTHEEK VOORUIT DE STEUR

The 5 best
STREET MARKETS

---

206 PRONDELMARKT

Sint-Jacobsmarkt
St-Jacobs Quarter ④

A lively flea market is held on a cobbled square behind the Sint-Jacobskerk on Friday, Saturday and Sunday mornings. The dealers set up stalls around 8 am selling ancient electrical appliances, crates of vinyl records, dusty vases and the occasional stuffed zebra. The mood is lively, with people shouting in Ghent dialect, customers grabbing an early breakfast on a café terrace and the smell of fried potatoes wafting over from Frituur Bij Sint-Jacobs.

207 KOUTER

Kouter
Central Ghent ①

Locals have been coming to the Kouter square on Sunday mornings to buy flowers since the 18th century. Some 15 different stallholders now set up colourful stands selling tulips and vivid Ghent azaleas grown in vast greenhouses outside the city. You can eat a plate of oysters at De Blauwe Kiosk or perch on a stool at La Dolce Barista's painted coffee van for a superb Italian espresso.

208 BOOK MARKET

Ajuinlei
Central Ghent ①

Dealers in secondhand books set up stalls along the Leie waterfront on Sunday mornings. The mood is relaxed as locals browse through the piles of old books and magazines, or stop off for a glass of white wine at l'Apéro d'Oc.

209 VRIJDAGMARKT

Vrijdagmarkt
St-Jacobs Quarter ④

Held every Friday morning on the Vrijdagmarkt, this street market is crammed with stalls selling fruit, cheese, shoes and stockings. You can count on at least one food van selling Italian pasta and a giant truck with its side opened up to reveal fresh sole, lobsters and herring.

210 BIOMARKT

Groentenmarkt
Central Ghent ①

A modest farmers' market is held every Friday morning on the Groentenmarkt. Here you find a few stands selling organic fruit and vegetables produced by small, sustainable farms in East Flanders.

209 VRIJDAGMARKT

TWIGGY

40 PLACES FOR FASHION AND DESIGN

The 5 most
CREATIVE FASHION STORES

---

211 TWIGGY

Notarisstraat 3
Central Ghent ①
+32 (0)9 223 95 66
www.twiggy.be

This inspiring fashion store for men and women moved in 2012 into a grand 19th-century town house radically remodelled by the Ghent architects de vylder vinck taillieu. The upstairs rooms have a romantic look with old marble fireplaces and mirrors, but the real excitement is down in the basement where a floor has been ripped out to leave a fireplace suspended in mid-air and a door leading nowhere. The store sells brands like Acne, Paul Smith and Isabel Marant.

212 LES FILLES ET LES CHIENS

Zuidstationstraat 9
University Quarter ⑥
+32 (0)9 336 39 51
lesfillesetleschiens.be

It's a bit of a walk from the centre, but worth it simply to look inside this inspiring store. It occupies a former hotel decorated with ornate 18th-century ceilings and painted doors. Owners Helen Wouters and Barbara Symons offer cups of tea and chocolates to nibble while you browse around. They stock edgy clothes, unusual jewellery and quirky accessories.

213 REWIND WOMEN

Sint-Pieters-
nieuwstraat 44
University Quarter ⑥
+32 (0)9 324 84 04
www.rewindstore.be

A cool shop that brings together interesting Scandinavian and French designers. You find clothes by Samsøe & Samsøe, Sessùn and Surface to Air, along with neat leather bags by Becksöndergaard.

214 EVA BOS

Vlaanderenstraat 66
Central Ghent ①
+32 (0)495 49 61 64

Designer Eva Bos presents her line of elegant women's clothing, made to measure, in a tiny but beautiful Art Deco boutique, decorated with mosaic floors and old theatre lamps. Right next door is her flower shop, Bos Bloemen.

215 A SUIVRE

Brabantdam 27
Central Ghent ①
+32 (0)9 233 99 92
www.asuivre.be

Women come to this store to seek out cool, sophisticated clothes in bold colours. You find the best Danish and French designers, along with Belgian brands like Just in Case.

214 EVA BOS

211 TWIGGY

The 5 most inspiring
GHENT DESIGNERS

---

216 BLACK BALLOON

Henegouwenstraat 85
Central Ghent ①
www.blackballoon.be

The Ghent fashion designers Cléo Baele and Sarah Bos create chic clothes and accessories. Sometimes they use black. Other times sunny colours prevail. Their fans include the Ghent band Soulwax and the Belgian rock star born in Ostend Arno.

217 JO DE VISSCHER

Hoornstraat 6
Central Ghent ①
+32 (0)9 233 88 04
www.jodevisscher.be

Jo de Visscher is one of the most exciting young designers in Belgium. She began her career as an art restorer but moved into fashion after Walter Van Beirendonck invited her to take part in an exhibition. She opened this shop in 2013 in a beautiful Art Deco interior.

218 ARAVINDA RODENBURG

Bagattenstraat 137
University Quarter ⑥
+32 (0)498 50 08 75
www.aravinda
rodenburg.be

Aravinda Rodenburg is an old-school tailor who creates classic bespoke suits in his Ghent workshop. He uses the best materials to create suits that are carefully designed down to the last button. His customers include artists and musicians willing to pay extra for something special.

219 LA FILLE D'O

Burgstraat 21
Patershol ②
+32 (0)9 334 80 10
lafilledo.com

The rebellious Ghent lingerie designer Murielle Scherre started her business selling sexy bras and knickers in her living room. She gradually built up a loyal following that includes celebrities like Lady Gaga and Rihanna. Now she has her own shop where she sells edgy lingerie and sometimes organises daring fashion shows in the window. Her videos are admired for using normal women rather than skinny fashion models.

220 MAYENNE (& RENÉE)

Hoogpoort 31
Central Ghent ①
+32 (0)488 57 37 00
www.mayenne-nelen.com

Mayenne Nelen has a tiny shop in the centre of Ghent where she sells leather shoulder bags, laptop bags and men's braces. She was joined in early 2014 by the young Ghent goldsmith Nele Braet who creates unique jewellery under the label Renée.

217 JO DE VISSCHER

The 5 places most loved by
FASHIONISTAS

---

221 PAND 13

Henegouwenstraat 13
Central Ghent ①
+32 (0)9 233 47 00

Ghent's fashionistas find cool garments in this beautiful old-fashioned store. It occupies two handsome buildings on one of the smartest streets in town. Here you find youthful and romantic clothes by labels like Paule Ka and See by Chloé.

222 HET OORCUSSEN

Vrijdagmarkt 7
St-Jacobs Quarter ④
+32 (0)9 233 07 65
www.oorcussen.be

This small and elegant store is hidden away among the restaurants and café terraces on Vrijdagmarkt. Yet the narrow 17th-century building is a fashionista's dream. The owner Caroline Naudts stocks Antwerp designers like Dries van Noten, Ann Demeulemeester and A.F. Vandevorst, along with casual chic clothes by French label Isabel Marant.

223 MIEKE

Baudelostraat 23
St-Jacobs Quarter ④
+32 (0)9 330 65 10
www.mieke.tv

It's a bit out of the way, but Mieke De Winter's shop is worth a visit. She spends her time tracking down clothes by unknown designers like Dear Creatures and Nancy Dee. Here is where young Ghent women find flirty dresses and shoes for late-night parties.

224 ZOOT

Serpentstraat 8
Central Ghent ①
+32 (0)9 233 70 75
www.zootcostumiers.be

Fashion hunters come to this friendly shop when they are looking for something fun and a little frivolous. Zoot stocks colourful clothes by brands like Fever and Who's That Girl, along with shoes in every colour by Noë of Antwerp.

225 ELLE ET GAND

Jan Palfijnstraat 36
St-Jacobs Quarter ④
+32 (0)9 234 23 33
www.elleetgand.be

Julie Huysman's boutique isn't well known, but it's worth tracking down this tiny shop with the clever name if you are looking for something different. She sells gorgeous clothes by young relatively unknown designers from Brussels, Ghent and Paris. The store also stocks cushions, lamps, paintings and jewellery.

225 ELLE ET GAND

The 5 best shops for
MEN'S FASHION

---

226 STRELLI.HOMME

Walpoortstraat 34
University Quarter ⑥
+32 (0)9 278 92 70
www.strelli-homme.com

Most Belgian men wear subdued tones of grey and black that blend in with the rainy Belgian climate. Not those who wear Olivier Strelli. The brand was created by Nissim Israel who grew up in the Belgian Congo. He developed a love of bold colours and delicate fabrics in the hot African sun.

227 CAFÉ COSTUME

Brabantdam 135
Central Ghent ①
+32 (0)9 225 63 23
www.cafecostume.com

This discreet shop specialises in affordable bespoke suits. Based on a concept developed in Antwerp, the shop has a clean vintage interior with old family photographs and a drinks table made from a recycled school desk.

228 REWIND MEN

Sint-Pieters-
nieuwstraat 13
University Quarter ⑥
+32 (0)9 324 84 04
www.rewindstore.be

Christophe Urbain's Rewind store for men sells clothes and accessories by creative Scandinavian designers. Down in the basement, a tiny concept store called Rewind B.L.C.K.+ is dedicated to black garments and accessories by designers like A.F. Vandevorst, The Last Conspiracy and Rick Owens.

229 **DON**

Henegouwenstraat 8
Central Ghent ①
+32 (0)9 330 87 88
www.dongent.be

The owner of this small boutique offers men a crisp 1950s look. The shirts are laid out on old cabinets while vintage accessories are displayed in open drawers. This is the perfect shop to find something a bit more sharp than the chain stores offer.

230 **CHAPELLERIE GELAUDE**

Normaalschool-
straat 2
Citadelpark ⑤
+32 (0)9 222 21 27
www.gelaude.be

The Gelaude family has been running this beautiful hat shop since 1893. The hats are displayed in handsome old wooden cupboards with glass doors. They mainly stock classic labels like Borsalino, Stetson and Panama, but you also find cool contemporary styles.

227 CAFÉ COSTUME

The 5 best shops for
ACCESSORIES

---

231 ELS ROBBERECHTS

Onderbergen 39
Central Ghent ①
+32 (0)498 10 31 97
elsrobberechts.be

Els Robberechts has been making stylish hats in her Ghent atelier since 2000. She displays her hats in a spacious interior, along with handbags and accessories by Belgian designers such as Els Jacobs and Alex Schrijvers.

232 SOME THING ELS

Nieuwland 1
St-Jacobs Quarter ④
+32 (0)472 61 23 29
www.some-thing-els.be

Els Jacobs creates unique shawls and scarves sitting at a knitting machine in a workshop overlooking the River Leie. Her creations are displayed on wooden shelves next to her work space. Some of the pieces are more like works of art.

233 M.A.R.T.H.A.

Onderbergen 19
Central Ghent ①
+32 (0)9 330 66 40

Clarice Bressinck studied fashion in Ghent before opening this appealing little shop. She sells solid necklaces, long woollen scarves and bags made from recycled fabrics. Her prices are more affordable than you might expect.

234 OBIUS

Meerseniersstraat 4
St-Jacobs Quarter ④
+32 (0)9 233 82 69
www.obius.be

Obius occupies an old brick house hidden down a side street off Vrijdagmarkt. It is worth tracking down if you are hunting for unique shoes by Belgian and Italian designers. The owner stocks stylish footwear by Belgian designers Ann Demeulemeester and Kris van Assche, along with international brands like Prada and Viktor & Rolf.

235 TOUCHÉ

Brabantdam 56
Central Ghent ①
+32 (0)9 233 14 22
www.touche-gent.be

Sofie Taillieu sells fashionable shoes in a grand 19th-century town house with a stylish white interior. She stocks labels that you don't find easily, along with bags and gloves to complete the look.

235 TOUCHÉ

The 5 best shops for
JEWELLERY

236 ELISA LEE

Hoogpoort 33
Central Ghent ①
+32 (0)9 329 08 78
www.elisa-lee.be

Elisabeth Leenknegt sells bright jewellery in a cool Nordic interior with pastel-coloured stools and quirky fashion photos. She comes from an artistic family of glass designers and uses hand-blown coloured glass in many of her creations. Most of her jewellery is made to order.

237 COOREMETERSHUYS

Graslei 12
Central Ghent ①
+32 (0)9 225 09 65
www.cooremetershuys.be

Here is an inspiring jewellery shop located in an ancient corn exchange on the Graslei waterfront. Stone steps take you down to a 13th-century vaulted cellar where unique necklaces are displayed along with bags, hats and scarves.

238 ZAHIA

Beverhoutplein 13
St-Jacobs Quarter ④
+32 (0)9 233 62 20
www.zahia.be

This little shop is located on the square where the flea market is held. It sells an eclectic range of beads and precious stones for making necklaces and ear-rings. Jewellery-making classes are held on Saturdays at a long wooden table in the back room.

239 EDELGEDACHT

Henegouwenstraat 89
Central Ghent ①
+32 (0)9 233 66 10
www.edelgedacht.be

Jan Vanhoutteghem creates exceptionally beautiful necklaces that are like modern art. He sells them in a handsome shop that looks like a gallery.

240 ONIS

Kwaadham 52
Central Ghent ①
+32 (0)486 76 25 82
www.onisjuwelen.be

Isabelle Onselaere displays her creations in a handsome 19th-century town house in a quiet corner of the old town. The interior is decorated in a sober style with white furniture and grey walls. She makes simple jewellery using gold, silver and precious stones. Her husband has an art gallery in the same house, and the couple also run a B&B.

240 **ONIS**

The 5 best

VINTAGE SHOPS

---

241 MARMOD

Brabantdam 136
Central Ghent ①
+32 (0)494 62 91 91

This is a stylish vintage shop where you find rare and wonderful clothes, along with belts, hats and bags. It's worth dropping in just to admire clothes displayed in old boxes and cabinets, surrounded by vintage typewriters and Barbie dolls.

242 HOUSE OF VINTAGE

Dampoortstraat 27
Dampoort ⑧
+32 (0)487 61 90 66

A small shop with racks of bright 1980s dresses, slightly used bags and almost-new leather boots. It is popular with local actors and students who can walk out with a party dress, a handbag and a wild pair of stilettos for just a few euro.

243 ALTERNATIEF

Baudelostraat 15
Central Ghent ①
+32 (0)9 233 23 11
www.alternatief-boetiek.be

Located in the antique quarter, Alternatief is the place to look for something a little different. They stock unusual fashion from the 1970s and 1980s along with some new clothes. This is somewhere to come if you are looking for a smart little handbag or a pair of bold sunglasses.

244 PATRICIA VINTAGE

Henegouwenstraat 75
Central Ghent ⓘ
+32 (0)9 223 03 01

Patricia was selling vintage clothes in Ghent long before anyone else. She displays hand-picked clothes in a relaxed interior decorated with photographs of Audrey Hepburn and vases of flowers. You find Yves Saint Laurent dresses and Chanel accessories, along with newer items by Miu Miu and Prada.

245 OLGA'S RETRO

Korte Meer 23
Central Ghent ⓘ
+32 (0)495 42 53 31
olgaretro.weebly.com

Olga Martens is a bit of a rebel. She opened her tiny retro shop at an age when most Belgians look forward to retirement. Her main passion is for flamboyant 1950s fashions by Dior and Chanel. You find polka dot party dresses, fur hats and the occasional crocodile leather handbag.

241 MARMOD

The 5 best shops for
KIDS CLOTHES

---

246 MONSTERS WITH AN ATTITUDE

Sluizeken 34
Patershol ②
+32 (0)9 234 00 07
www.monsterswith
anattitude.be

This is a fun shop to seek out unusual clothes for little kids. Everything is colourful and frivolous, like orange woolly hats that look like chickens and bibs with animal faces. Just the place if you are searching for an unusual gift for a newborn.

247 PETIT ZSA-ZSA

Serpentstraat 5
Central Ghent ①
+32 (0)9 224 45 74
www.zsazsarouge.be/
petitszasza

A fun shop for kids' clothes run by the same people as Pink Flamingo's and Zsa-Zsa Rouge. Everything comes in bright colours with fun details.

248 MENEER JANSSEN EN JUFFROUW KAAT

Gouvernementstraat 7
Central Ghent ①
+32 (0)9 269 05 13
www.misterjonesand
misskatie.be

Véronique Vandriessche opened this inspiring store for kids' fashions in 2000. She stocks exclusive clothes by brands like Max & Lola, Bellerose and Paul Smith. The shop is run by an exceptionally friendly young team who can advise on size, colour and anything else you need to know.

249 AAP.NOOT.MIES

Bennesteeg 1
Central Ghent ①
+32 (0)9 224 06 00
www.aapnootmies.be

This small shop selling kids' shoes is named after the first three words that Dutch-speaking children learn at school. An old photograph taken at a Belgian girls' boarding school hangs on the wall above rows of sensible shoes for small children.

250 PASTEM HOMEMADE T-SHIRTS & HOODIES

Bennesteeg 12
Central Ghent ①

You can't miss this shop. It has a huge mural on the outside wall by the Ghent street artist Bué the Warrior. The owner sells bright T-shirts and hoodies printed with cartoons. Kids love the concept.

249 AAP.NOOT.MIES

WEAVERS CHAPEL

30 BUILDINGS TO ADMIRE

The 5 strangest
LOST AND ABANDONED CHURCHES

---

251 THE GREEN CHURCH

Voorhoutkaai 43
Dampoort ⑧
+32 (0)9 225 96 44
burenvandeabdij.be

The old abbey church of Sint-Baafs has vanished. It was demolished by the Spanish in the 16th-century, leaving behind an empty space. But then in 2006 the city gardens department decided to plant tall clipped hornbeam bushes to mark the outline of the vanished 12th-century church.

252 KAPEL DRONGENHOF

Drongenhof
Patershol ②

The early 17th-century Drongenhof Chapel is a sad, abandoned place. It is sometimes used for concerts and exhibitions, but normally stays locked. Yet you can peer through the gap between the green doors to glimpse a modern stained glass window at the far end. Installed in 2003 by the Ghent artist Wim Delvoye, it is decorated with X-ray pictures of couples having sex.

253 WEAVERS' CHAPEL

Kortedagsteeg 12
Central Ghent ①

From the outside, McGregor's looks like any other chain store. But you are in for a surprise when you step through the door. The shop occupies a former 14th-century chapel with whitewashed walls and a high vaulted roof. Built for the Guild of Wool Weavers, the chapel has served in the past as a cinema, reading room and garage. It was converted into a shop in 2002 by the Antwerp architect Christine Conix.

254 KAPEL BAUDELOO

Ottogracht 2
St-Jacobs Quarter ④

A strange late-gothic chapel lies almost hidden behind a classical portico on Ottogracht. Once part of the Baudeloo Abbey, the chapel was converted into a library in 1880, but now lies abandoned and forgotten. The baroque spire and roof are all that can be seen until some inspiring new purpose can be found for the building.

255 GALERIE ST-JOHN

Bij Sint-Jacobs 15a
St-Jacobs Quarter ④
+32 (0)9 225 82 62
www.st-john.be

A disused baroque church near Sint-Jacobskerk was converted into an antique store in 1980. It is crammed with old books, piles of prints, boxes of cutlery and odd statues. Most of it is sold at auction, but some small items can be bought on the spot. Go down to the crypt to look at paintings by Belgian artists, and don't leave without looking at the huge Surrealist painting suspended from the organ loft.

The 5 most striking
MODERN BUILDINGS

---

256 STADSHAL

Emile Braunplein
Central Ghent ①

Some local people call it the sheep shed. Others consider it a sublime modern building. The controversial Stadshal doesn't leave anyone indifferent. It was designed in 2012 by the partnership Robbrecht & Daem and Marie-José Van Hee to serve as a modern covered hall for concerts and events. It may have its critics, but it has won several architectural prizes for its daring design.

257 STUDIO S3

Bijlokekaai 1
Bijloke Quarter ③
+32 (0)9 221 75 01
www.lesballetscdela.be

The Ghent architects de vylder vinck taillieu have created some inspiring buildings in Ghent, including the interior of Twiggy. But their most striking project is the new dance studio designed in 2008 for Les Ballets C de la B. Located next to the old Bijloke hospital, the studio has a glass side wall that reveals a staircase made from recycled wood.

258 FACULTY OF ECONOMICS BUILDING

Tweekerkenstraat 2
University Quarter ⑥

It's worth taking a look around this multilayered university building built by Xaveer De Geyter and Stéphane Beel. Constructed in 2006-10, the building occupies a sloping site where an old path once ran down to the river.

259 TICHELREI 100

Tichelrei 100
Patershol ②

The Ghent architects de vylder vinck taillieu built this contemporary house on an empty plot of land. It blends in with the rest of the street and yet brings something fresh to urban living.

260 NEW ZEBRA

Zebrastraat 32
University Quarter ⑥
+32 (0)471 31 00 01
www.zebrastraat.be

This striking project completed in 2013 incorporates a circular 19th-century workers' housing complex and a new building with a convex façade. The development includes apartments, a restaurant and an exhibition space.

256 STADSHAL

The 5 most
IMPRESSIVE TOWERS

---

261 ST-NIKLAASTOREN
Emile Braunplein
Central Ghent ①

The oldest of Ghent's three towers, the Sint-Niklaastoren, was built in the 13th century in a sober early gothic style. The stone tower can be spotted in the middle panel of the Ghent Altarpiece amid a cluster of Gothic church spires.

262 BELFORT
Emile Braunplein
Central Ghent ①

The ancient stone belfry has a lift to take you to the top. Here you get a sweeping view down onto the roofs of the old city. The belfry was begun in 1314, but the ornate spire is a recent addition, built in 1911-13 for the Ghent World Fair. It was modelled on a 14th-century drawing, while the dragon at the top was copied from an ancient weather vane.

263 SINT-BAAFSTOREN
Sint-Baafsplein
Central Ghent ①

The 89-metre west tower of Sint-Baafs Cathedral was built between 1462 and 1538 in Brabant gothic style. It once had a spire that was destroyed in a fire, leaving the tower looking rather austere.

264 BOEKENTOREN

Rozier 9
University Quarter ⑥
+32 (0)9 264 38 51
www.boekentoren.be

Built on the highest point in the city, the Boekentoren (Book Tower) is a striking modernist building by the Belgian architect Henry van de Velde. Designed in 1933, the 24-floor concrete tower is occupied by the university's vast collection of books. It is seen as the city's fourth tower.

265 WATER TOWER

Kattenberg 2
University Quarter ⑥

A curious glass water tower was built in 1977 on high ground near the Boekentoren. It stands next to two older water towers dating from 1881 that are no longer in use. The wavy glass tower was designed to be virtually invisible by reflecting the surrounding buildings. It is now occupied by the university bike hire service.

262 BELFORT

The 5 most beautiful
ART NOUVEAU
HOUSES

---

266 HOECKE-DESSEL HOUSE
Kunstlaan 41
Citadelpark ⑤

The architect Achilles Van Hoecke-Dessel built a number of Art Nouveau houses on the leafy avenue Kunstlaan. But the finest house in the street is undoubtedly the one he designed for himself in 1903. It may seem rather sober until you look at the gorgeous circular frame around the door and the elegant ironwork on the balconies.

267 PRINSES CLEMENTINALAAN 20
Prinses
Clementinalaan 20
Station Quarter ⑦

It is worth taking a walk along the lovely Prinses Clementinalaan in southern Ghent to look at the beautiful Art Nouveau houses decorated with glazed bricks, horseshoe windows, bay windows and tile pictures. The most striking is No. 20, which was built in 1910 by the architect Urbain Crommen as his home and office. The Villa Elisabeth at No. 86 was designed in a similar style by Leon De Keyser.

268 **FORTLAAN 17**

Fortlaan 17
Station Quarter ⑦
+32 (0)9 222 00 33
www.fortlaan17.com

Five years after the first Art Nouveau house was built in Brussels, the Ghent architect Beert Campens brought the style to Ghent. He created a beautiful house opposite the Citadelpark in 1899 with fin-de-siècle details such as whiplash decoration, ornate ironwork and delicate flowers etched onto sgraffito panels. The house is now used as a gallery, exhibiting works by various artists.

269 **PARKLAAN 39**

Parklaan 39
Station Quarter ⑦

The architect Jules-Pascal Ledoux designed a slender Art Nouveau house facing the Citadelpark in 1900. It has a beautiful carved door and several painted tile pictures.

270 **VERNIERS HOUSE**

Sluizeken 8
Patershol ②
simonsays.be

This eccentric Art Nouveau corner house was built by Georges Henderick in 1904. The architect took some familiar Art Nouveau motifs such as arched windows and carved wood, but added an exotic touch with his striking use of colour. Repainted in its original colours in 1994, the building is now occupied by Simon Says, a cool coffee shop and B&B.

The 5 most
UNUSUAL HOUSES

---

271 THE CAT AND THE DOG
Leopold II-laan 24
Citadelpark ⑤

Look out for the curious house known as De Kat en de Hond (The Cat and the Dog) built in 1903 opposite the Citadelpark. Designed by the architect Louis Cloquet, this grand mansion has a brick stair tower, a glass-roofed entrance hall and an elaborate neo-gothic letter box. But the oddest details are the little sculptures to the left of the door showing a cat fighting a dog.

272 KANUNNIKSTRAAT
Kanunnikstraat 2
University Quarter ⑥

The side wall of a corner house on the route of tram 1 is covered with bizarre metal sculptures and faded murals showing episodes from Ghent's history, including a biplane flying over the city's towers. Other odd details on this mysterious house include a metal bird pecking in a bowl.

273 **MOLENAARSSTRAAT 43**

Molenaarsstraat 43
Patershol ②

Molenaarsstraat is a typical Ghent street lined with terraced workers' houses. But No. 43 stands out. The Ghent artist Leo Coppens covered the façade with fluorescent military camouflage to create the work *The True Hero Command Post*.

274 **HUIS DE PASSER**

Wolfstraat 12
St-Jacobs Quarter ④

It's worth walking down the quiet side street where Jacob Semey built several Flemish Renaissance houses in 1908. The most striking is De Passer (The Compass) which is richly ornamented with Renaissance details along with an Old Dutch proverb. Most of the other houses in this street were designed by the same architect. Several have terracotta reliefs that illustrate the house name, such as The Wolf at No. 3, Romulus and Remus at No. 9 and The Sturgeon at No. 13.

275 **WELKOM**

Sint-Pieters-
nieuwstraat 108
University Quarter ⑥

Several old shops have decorative mosaic floors with the old name of the shop picked out in tiny marble squares. You can see an impressive example with the word Salve (Welcome) in front of an Art Nouveau apartment building facing Vooruit. It was built by the architect Pol Hoste in 1917 while Ghent was under German Occupation. The word *Welkom* is carved in a stone above the door.

The 5 most
CURIOUS BUILDINGS

---

276 WINTER CIRCUS

Sint-Pieters-
nieuwstraat 9
University Quarter ⑥

Many people have never been inside the huge circus hidden behind the shops on Sint-Pietersnieuwstraat. The top of the dome can just be seen from the street corner outside No. 108. The circus was built in 1893 and reconstructed after a fire in 1920. It once staged huge circus shows for audiences of 3,400, but the vast circular space now lies empty and abandoned. The city now has plans to develop the building as a concert hall.

277 MASONS' GUILD HOUSE

Cataloniëstraat 1
Central Ghent ①

The Masons' Guild House was built in a flamboyant gothic style opposite the Sint-Niklaaskerk to show off the stone carving skills of the city's masons. It eventually disappeared behind a later building. People thought it had been demolished and so in 1913 a replica was constructed at Graslei 8. The original was later found during building work and six modern dancing figures were added at the top.

278 VENETIAN FAÇADES
Lammerstraat 1
University Quarter ⑥

Not many people notice the curious white façade in the Lammerstraat built in Venetian Gothic style. It was constructed in 1851 to provide a single façade for six shops. Nothing has survived at street level, but the upper two floors have retained the strange Venetian windows and Byzantine details.

279 HET PIANOHUIS
Stoppelstraat 35
Bijloke Quarter ③

This curious corner house was built in 2007 as a guest house for pianists. The architect designed the oddly shaped windows to suggest the shape of a grand piano.

280 BELGACOM BUILDING
Keizer Karelstraat
Central Ghent ①

The Belgacom building was once voted the ugliest building in Ghent. You may agree with the verdict when you see the grey concrete block built for the national telecom company in the 1970s. It was scheduled to be demolished some years ago, but is somehow still standing.

277 MASONS' GUILD HOUSE

SINT-PIETERSABDIJ GARDEN

PROVENIERSSTERSSTRAAT

55 PLACES TO DISCOVER GHENT

———

The 5 most
UNEXPECTED VIEWS

---

281 MIAT MUSEUM
Minnemeers 9
Patershol ②
+32 (0)9 269 42 00
www.miat.gent.be

Most people climb the belfry for a view of the city, but there are other more unexpected views of the old town. The most surprising comes on the top floor of the MIAT industrial museum where you can look south through the old cotton mill windows.

282 GELDMUNT
Geldmunt 1
Central Ghent ①

Ghent is a mysterious city of meandering rivers that emerge in unexpected places. Some spots along the river are well known, like the Appelpark on Jan Breydelstraat, but there are a few places where you can be totally alone, like the area of grass reached down a lane off Geldmunt.

283 SINT-WIDOSTRAAT
Sint-Widostraat 4
Patershol ②

Not many people walk down the old lane called Sint-Widostraat, but it leads to an attractive spot on the waterfront just beyond the small NTGent Arca theatre. Here you get an unexpected view of the River Leie and the Gravensteen.

284 TOURIST OFFICE BENCH

Sint-Veerleplein 5
Central Ghent ⓘ
+32 (0)9 266 56 60
www.visitgent.be

The Ghent tourist office moved in 2012 from a dark basement room below the Belfry into a stunning glass box next to the old fish market. You can sit on a stylish modern bench overlooking the river for a striking view of the old town. The perfect spot to sit on a rainy day, with free wifi if you need to keep up with things.

285 HOSTEL UPPELINK, ROOM 10

Sint-Michielsplein 21
Central Ghent ⓘ
+32 (0)9 279 44 77
hosteluppelink.com

The room with the best view in Ghent is located in a cheap hostel that opened in 2013. Room 10 in the Hostel Uppelink has five single beds, a table and a couple of chairs. It's very basic accommodation, but the view from the bedroom window is stunning. We think this could be the coolest place to stay in Ghent.

281 MIAT

The 5 best places to
understand the
HISTORY OF GHENT

---

286 STAM

Godshuizenlaan 2
Bijloke Quarter ③
+32 (0)9 267 14 00
www.stamgent.be

Ghent's city history museum is located in a restored mediaeval abbey with a stunning Gothic refectory. The museum was brilliantly renovated in 2010 by the Ghent city architect Koen Van Nieuwenhuyse. The first room now has an enormous map of the city laid out in the floor, while other rooms use interactive maps, sound recordings and contemporary photographs by Carl De Keyzer to create an exceptional portrait of one of Europe's most fascinating cities.

287 SINT-PIETERSABDIJ

Sint-Pietersplein 9
University Quarter ⑥
+32 (0)9 243 97 30
sintpietersabdijgent.be

A handheld video takes you on an unusual tour through the huge abbey of Sint-Pieters in the footsteps of a fictional monk with Scottish roots called Jean François Alison. You climb countless winding stairs during the 90-minute tour, which takes in the organ loft in the baroque church and the dark attic hidden above the refectory. It is a fascinating way to discover an ancient abbey.

288 GRAVENSTEEN

Sint-Veerleplein 11
Central Ghent ①
+32 (0)9 225 93 06
www.gravensteengent.be

An ancient stone castle dating from the 12th century stands right in the centre of Ghent. It is a fascinating mediaeval building with dark winding staircases, gloomy dungeons and a creepy torture chamber. Visitors can pick up an iTouch to watch a fictional mediaeval story unfold as they roam through the 15 rooms. But it is possibly enough to wander through this ancient stone building without any further commentary. The views from the battlements are spectacular.

289 SINT-BAAFSABDIJ RUINS

Voorhoutkaai 43
Dampoort ⑧
+32 (0)9 225 96 44
burenvandeabdij.be

Not many people know about the ruined Sint-Baafsabdij near Portus Ganda. One of the great abbeys of the middle ages, it was largely demolished by the Spanish in the 16th century, but a few fragments including a spectacular mediaeval refectory have survived. The ruins are dotted with stone columns, doorways, and sculptures salvaged from demolished Ghent buildings. The site is kept open by volunteers, but only in the summer months for a few days each week.

290 MUNTENROUTE

Donkersteeg
Central Ghent ①
www.visitgent.be

You have to look hard to notice the little bronze medallions set in the paving stones in the city centre. These mysterious objects are engraved with old hotel bills, views of vanished buildings, historical documents and ancient coins. The architects Robbrecht and Daem came up with the idea of creating a Muntenroute, or Coin Trail, while they were redesigning the city centre. Some 1,000 coins are laid in the paving along the old trading route from Ghent to Cologne. One group of coins in the Donkersteeg shows details of old hotels.

288 ,GRAVENSTEEN

287 SINT-PIETERSABDIJ

The 5 most interesting
BRIDGES

---

291 **ST-MICHIELSBRUG**
St.-Michielshelling
Central Ghent ①

The St.-Michielsbrug was built across the River Leie from 1905 to 1909. It was designed in neo-gothic style by Louis Cloquet who also built the nearby post office. The view from the bridge takes in the Graslei waterfront and the three Ghent towers.

292 **LIEVEBRUG**
Lievebrug
Patershol ②

This little bridge across the River Lieve is one of the most romantic spots in Ghent, with houses rising out of the water to the south and weeping willow trees lining the banks to the north. Yet almost no one ever comes here.

293 **SLACHTHUISBRUG**
Slachthuisbrug
Dampoort ⑧
www.portusganda.be

The Leie opens out into a large harbour known as Portus Ganda crossed by the Slachthuisbrug. The city has constructed a wooden deck projecting into the water with rows of benches where you can admire the view. Locals call the spot 'the bows of the Titanic'.

294 THE BRIDGE OF THE EMPEROR'S PLEASURES

Sint-Antoniuskaai
Patershol ②

Walter De Buck created a strange set of four sculptures to decorate a small bridge across the Lieve. They are said to illustrate various episodes from the life of Charles V, but locals prefer to call them the *krimbollen*, or ice cream cones.

295 APPELBRUG

Jan Breydelstraat 8
Central Ghent ①

A new footbridge was built across the narrow River Lieve to connect with the back of the Vismarkt. Not many people stand on this bridge, yet it has one of the best views of the old city. You see several historic building from unusual angles, including the rugged stone Vleeshal, the Vishal rising out of the water like a ship and the backs of old houses on Jan Breydelstraat.

291 ST-MICHIELSBRUG

The 5 most
SURPRISING PLAQUES

296 THE TREATY OF GHENT
Veldstraat 47
Central Ghent ①

One of the most surprising plaques in Ghent is attached to the wall of the Esprit store. It marks the site of a building where a delegation of five Americans, led by John Quincy Adams, stayed between July and December 1814. They had travelled to Ghent of all places to negotiate a peace treaty with Britain to end the War of Independence. A small plaque below was put up in 1964 by the Daughters of the Revolution 'in appreciation of the hospitality of the people of Ghent.'

297 EDITH CAVELL
Kortrijkse-
steenweg 128
Station Quarter ⑦

A dusty bronze plaque set in the wall of an apartment building recalls the story of the nurse Edith Cavell who was executed in Brussels for helping British soldiers to escape during the First World War. 'The glorious victim of German barbarity was secretly harboured in this house in April 1915,' the plaque says.

298 PIERRE DE GEYTER
Kanunnikstraat 8
University Quarter ⑥

A rustic wooden plaque on a house in the student quarter recalls that the composer Pierre de Geyter was born in the neighbourhood in 1848. His most famous work was the socialist Internationale which he composed in 1888. He was invited to Moscow by Stalin in 1927 to take part in celebrations to mark the anniversary of the October Revolution.

299 ALBRECHT DÜRER
Klein Turkije 4
Central Ghent ①

An old bronze plaque with a Gothic inscription is attached to the ancient stone house overlooking the St.-Niklaas-kerk. It records that the German painter Albrecht Dürer spent a week here in 1521 staying at De Rode Hoed (The Red Hat). Dürer climbed the Sint-Baafs tower, sketched a lion in the Prinsenhof and looked at the Van Eyck altarpiece, which he described as a 'stupendous and highly intelligent painting'.

300 HUGO VAN DER GOES
Sint-Pieters-nieuwstraat 158
University Quarter ⑥

A bronze plaque on a building opposite Vooruit marks the building where the Ghent artist Hugo van der Goes painted the famous Portinari Altarpiece. The work, which depicts the Adoration of the Magi, was commissioned by the Italian banker Tommaso Portinari in 1473 to hang in a chapel in Florence. The artist suffered a breakdown soon after it was completed.

The 5 most
INSPIRING MUSEUMS

301 **MUSEUM DR. GUISLAIN**

Jozef Guislain-
straat 43
Western Ghent
+32 (0)9 216 35 95
museumdrguislain.be

Here is a strange and haunting museum on the edge of town. It occupies one wing of a model psychiatric institution founded in the 19th century by Dr. Jozef Guislain. Visitors can wander through chilling deserted wards still furnished with iron beds and old medical equipment. One room contains a terrifying mechanical saw used in operations to remove the top of the skull. The temporary exhibitions are always fascinating, as is the extensive collection of outsider art. Almost no one leaves this museum untouched.

302 **HUIS VAN ALIJN**

Kraanlei 65
Central Ghent ①
+32 (0)9 269 23 50
www.huisvanalijn.be

This captivating museum of local life is located in a 14th-century almshouse on the Leie waterfront. The 77 tiny almshouses are filled with old toys, funeral relics, reconstructed shop interiors and pigeon racing mementoes. The museum also has a collection of family snapshots and home movies from the 1960s, as well as a puppet theatre and an old Flemish tavern where you can drink a Ghent beer.

303 DESIGN MUSEUM

Jan Breydelstraat 5
Central Ghent ①
+32 (0)9 267 99 99
designmuseumgent.be

One of the world's most inspiring design collections lies hidden behind an 18th-century mansion. The older rooms have creaking wooden floors and historic furniture, including a magnificent wooden chandelier and two armchairs owned by Catherine the Great. But the real delight of this museum lies in the modern building added at the back by the Ghent architect Willy Verstraete in 1992. Here you find several sublime Art Nouveau rooms along with striking modern objects acquired for the collection by the director Lieven Daenens.

304 S.M.A.K.

N. De Liemaeckere-
plein 2
Citadelpark ⑤
+32 (0)9 240 76 01
www.smak.be

Ghent's contemporary art museum opened in 1999 in the Citadelpark with a boxing match organised by the curator Jan Hoet. The museum organises temporary exhibitions in a series of white rooms, as well as major art events that can take over the entire city.

305 MIAT

Minnemeers 9
Patershol ②
+32 (0)9 269 42 00
www.miat.gent.be

Located in an old textile mill, MIAT is an inspiring museum of Ghent factory life with an impressive collection of industrial relics. The most striking feature is a reconstructed textile factory floor with rows of working machines that create a deafening noise during demonstrations.

The 5 most
SECRET STREETS

---

306 TURREPOORTSTEEG

Turrepoortsteeg
Central Ghent ①

A forgotten lane runs between high brick walls off the Hoogstraat. It takes its name from the 13th-century Turrepoort city gate that once stood here. The lane passes below an old white house decorated with a religious shrine containing a little Virgin and Child lit by two lamps.

307 BIEZEKAPELSTRAAT

Biezekapelstraat
Central Ghent ①

Only a few people walk down this crooked lane hidden behind the Cathedral. But it is one of the best places to feel something of the menace of 14th-century Ghent when wealthy families lived in massive stone houses. The Ghent music academy now occupies several of these old buildings. Some-times you can hear a Beethoven sonata or a student practising on the violin as you pass this way.

308 PROVENIERSTERS-STRAAT

Proveniersterstraat
Patershol ②

This old cobbled lane is one of the most beautiful spots in Ghent. It is lined with whitewashed houses that once belonged to the St.-Elisabeth Begijnhof. The doorways still have iron grilles, bell-pulls and small statues of saints, but the protective wall that enclosed the Begijnhof was demolished in the 19th century.

309 PARIJSBERG

Parijsberg
University Quarter ⑥

This narrow side street runs down to the Leie waterfront, past the Vooruit stage entrance. Sometimes the lane is blocked by a truck unloading musical instruments. But it is worth squeezing past to look at the street art sprayed on the walls by Bué and other artists.

310 WELLINGSTRAAT

Wellingstraat
Central Ghent ①

This quiet side street is lined with modest 16th and 17th-century houses where textile workers once lived. Several houses have step gables and small religious shrines attached to the wall.

308 PROVENIERSTERSSTRAAT

The 5 most interesting
NEIGHBOURHOODS

---

311 PATERSHOL
Patershol ②

This old quarter of narrow alleys and brick houses was settled in the 10th century by leather workers. It became a notorious slum in the 20th century, populated by criminal gangs and prostitutes. But the city began a major renovation in the 1980s and Patershol is now an attractive old quarter occupied by restaurants, bars and galleries.

312 PRINSENHOF
Patershol ②

It was once the site of a great palace, but the Prinsenhof neighbourhood is now almost forgotten. You can wander here along empty cobbled lanes lined with brick houses from the 17th century and occasionally come across a deserted stretch of the River Lieve.

313 DOK NOORD
Koopvaardijlaan
Dampoort ⑧
+32 (0)9 224 19 40
dokgent.be

The abandoned Ghent docks to the north of the city are slowly being transformed into a new urban quarter. The old quays provide a striking setting in the summer for rock concerts, art exhibitions, film screenings, pop up restaurants and a cool urban beach.

314 **PORTUS GANDA**
Dampoort ⑧

The old port area to the east of the old town lies at the confluence of the Leie and the Scheldt. It used to be a run-down neighbourhood, but the city has transformed it into a lively waterfront district with restored quaysides and moorings for small boats. Look out for the tiny blue summer bar called Kiosko at the end of Hagelandkaai.

315 **MILJOENENKWARTIER**
Paul de Smet
de Naeyerplein
Station Quarter ⑦

Follow Krijgslaan under the railway line and you come to a quarter of grand villas overlooking a romantic park. Known as the Miljoenenkwartier (Millions' District), it was built in the 1920s on the site of the 1913 World Fair. Several local architects created distinctive villas in Art Deco style for Ghent's élite.

311 PATERSHOL

312 PRINSENHOF

The 5 most
SECRET GARDENS

---

316 SINT-PIETERSABDIJ
Sint-Pietersplein 12
University Quarter ⑥
+32 (0)9 243 97 30
sintpietersabdijgent.be

A secret garden lies hidden behind the Sint-Pietersabdij on the slopes above the River Scheldt. Entered by an old coach gate, this romantic spot dates back to the 9th century when the hillside was terraced to create a vineyard. The site was restored in 1983 and replanted with fruit trees, vines and herbs. It is popular with students, but sometimes you have the place to yourself. Not open on Mondays.

317 VEERGREP
Kortrijksepoort-
straat 196
Bijloke Quarter ③

Ghent students bring their textbooks to study in this secret little park. Created in 1992 on a patch of sloping land leading down to the River Leie, it feels romantic and even a little bit wild.

318 SINT-LUCAS SCULPTURE COURTYARD

Zwartezusterstraat 34
Central Ghent ①

The inner courtyard of the Sint-Lucas Academy is filled with a strange, forgotten collection of Gothic and Baroque fragments. They were placed here in the 19th century when this building, formerly a monastery, was turned into an art academy. The arches, gargoyles and doorways were once used to teach the principles of architecture, but they are now overgrown with moss.

319 D'HANE-STEENHUYSE GARDEN

Korte Meer 20a
Central Ghent ①

Not many people notice the coach entrance on the narrow back street Korte Meer. But it is worth taking a look inside if the door is open. You pass through an old stable block with a wooden hay rack and then enter a hidden 18th-century garden overlooked by the grand D'Hane-Steenhuyse Mansion. This is a strangely secret spot in the middle of Ghent.

320 PLANTENTUIN

Ledeganckstraat 35
Citadelpark ⑤
www.plantentuin-gent.be

Not many people ever take a look at the university botanical garden. Maybe it looks too serious and scientific, but it has a fascinating collection of 7,000 species from all over the world, along with an Alpine garden, tropical greenhouses and a romantic lake bordered with magnolias. The perfect spot to sit with a book in the summer.

319 D'HANE-STEENHUYSE

320 PLANTENTUIN

322 DE POT OP

The 5 strangest
URBAN DETAILS

321 DULLE GRIET
Grootkanonplein
Central Ghent ①

An enormous red wrought iron cannon stands near the Vrijdagmarkt. Constructed in the early 15th century, it was considered one of the most formidable weapons in mediaeval Europe. Named Dulle Griet after a legendary mad woman in Flemish folklore, it was only fired once during a siege in the 16th century when the heavy cannonball fell harmlessly to the ground.

322 DE POT OP
Jan Breydelstraat 5
Central Ghent ①
+32 (0)9 267 99 99
designmuseumgent.be

The designer Laude van Pee created a strange and controversial toilet in a courtyard at the back of the Design Museum. Named *De Pot Op* (On the toilet), it looks like a giant roll of toilet paper. Lit up at night, it can be seen from Drabstraat.

323 HORSE AND DOG FOUNTAINS

OPPOSITE
Kraanlei 25
Central Ghent ①
OPPOSITE
Vrijdagmarkt 42
Central Ghent ①

The city has preserved a couple of curious cast iron drinking fountains decorated with dogs, horses and birds. They were placed on the streets in the 19th century by the Society for the Protection of Animals. Look closely and you will see that they have three drinking bowls – one at the bottom for dogs, one higher up for horses and a third one at the top for birds.

324 BUNKERS

Jozef Kluyskensstraat
Bijloke Quarter ③

Two concrete bunkers covered with grass are still standing in the grounds of the former Bijloke hospital. Used as air raid shelters for hospital patients and nurses during the Second World War, these mysterious structures are now occupied by bat colonies.

325 DE GENTSE BARGE

Koophandelsplein
Central Ghent ①
+32 (0)473 48 26 59
www.gentsebarge.be

The most beautiful boat in Ghent is moored outside the old law courts. The gorgeous white and gold barge is a modern reconstruction of the 17th-century barges that sailed on the canal between Bruges and Ghent. The replica was made by the Ghent artist Walter De Buck working alongside local unemployed people.

The 5 most mysterious places in the
CITADELPARK

---

326 CITADEL GATE

Gustaaf
Den Duitsdreef
Citadelpark ⑤

The Citadelpark stands on the site of a massive fortress built by the British after the Battle of Waterloo. The fortifications were torn down in 1898 to create a romantic park, leaving just one surviving gate with the British army motto *Nemo me impune lacessit*.

327 MYSTERIOUS GROTTO

Norbert
Rousseaudreef
Citadelpark ⑤

The city embarked on a bizarre project in the 19th century to create an artificial mountain landscape on the site of the demolished fortress. The concrete rock formations incorporate a large grotto and a dramatic rocky route known as the Swiss Valley where mysterious doors are cut into the rocks.

328 AIR-RAID SHELTER

Théodore
Canneelpad
Citadelpark ⑤

Several derelict concrete ventilation shafts can be spotted in the trees above the Swiss Valley, next to a white building. They form part of a vast underground military bunker built in 1938. Used as an air raid shelter in the Second World War, it was converted into a military command post during the Cold War, but is now used by the city parks department simply to store their gardening tools.

329 BANDSTAND
Norbert
Rousseaudreef
Citadelpark ⑤

An elegant wrought iron bandstand was built in 1885 by the city architect Charles Van Rysselberghe. A relaxed jazz festival is held here in the summer.

330 OPEN-AIR THEATRE
Theodore
Canneelpad
Citadelpark ⑤

Only a few people in Ghent know about the open-air theatre built in the Citadelpark in 1945. Designed to seat 1,340 spectators, it now lies abandoned and forgotten among the trees.

327 MYSTERIOUS GROTTO

The 5 most
PEACEFUL SPOTS

---

331 KLEIN BEGIJNHOF

Lange Violette-
straat 77
University Quarter ⑥

The Small Begijnhof is a strangely deserted place hidden behind a high brick wall. A narrow cobbled lane leads into a settlement of neat gabled houses with little statues of saints above the doors. The houses were once occupied by single women, but many now lie abandoned.

332 PRINSENHOF

Prinsenhofplein
Patershol ②

Almost no one ever comes to this beautiful little square in the north of the city, yet this leafy spot was once the courtyard of the magnificent 15th-century Prinsenhof where Charles V was born in 1500. Nothing now remains of the palace except for a solitary gate. Even the scale model that once stood on a plinth has been stolen.

333 PRUDENS VAN DUYSEPLEIN

Prudens Van Duyse-
plein
Bijloke Quarter ③

The most beautiful tree in Ghent stands in a little park in the middle of a quiet roundabout. The plane tree was planted in 1700 at the spot where five roads met and later enclosed by a round hedge. It is one of the most romantic spots we know in Ghent.

334 HOF VAN RYHOVE

Onderstraat 22
Central Ghent ①

People rarely go through the small gate that leads into the Hof van Ryhove. This is one of the most peaceful spots in the city, except when children at the nearby school spill out into the playground. Once a 14th-century fortified house, its high walls conceal a secret garden replanted in mediaeval style with square plots and ancient varieties of pear trees.

335 MUINKPARK

Muinklaan
University Quarter ⑥

This was once the site of Ghent's zoo, but the animals vanished a long time ago, leaving behind a romantic little city park with winding paths and a small pond. Several houses overlooking the square were built in the 1920s in a striking Art Deco style.

331 KLEIN BEGIJNHOF

45 PLACES
TO ENJOY CULTURE

The 5 best places to see the
VAN EYCK ALTARPIECE

336 VILLA CHAPEL
Sint-Baafsplein
Central Ghent ①

The Van Eyck Altarpiece has been stolen, dismantled and hidden many times since it was unveiled in 1432, but it is now back in the Cathedral, complete apart from one panel stolen in 1934. It used to hang in the Vijd Chapel, but was moved in 1986 to the Villa Chapel, where it is displayed in a secure glass box.

337 ROOM 4, MUSEUM VOOR SCHONE KUNSTEN
Fernand Scribedreef 1
Citadelpark ⑤
+32 (0)9 240 07 00
www.mskgent.be

A major project to restore the 24 panels of Ghent Altarpiece is due to run from 2012 to 2017. The Altarpiece will be dismantled in stages and the panels restored in the Fine Arts Museum in southern Ghent. The restorers can be observed from Monday to Friday working in a room with a glass wall. It is fascinating to watch the experts using tiny scalpels to remove the dirt, and applying new paint with brushes that have just a single hair.

338 **CAERMERSKLOOSTER**
Vrouwebroersstraat 6
Central Ghent ①
+32 (0)9 269 29 10
www.caermersklooster.be

An exhibition on the Ghent Altarpiece occupies several rooms in an old Carmelite convent dating from 1329. The exhibition includes a link to a webcam installed in Room 4 at the Fine Arts Museum where panels are being lovingly restored.

339 **ROOM 6, STAM**
Godshuizenlaan 2
Bijloke Quarter ③
+32 (0)9 267 14 00
www.stamgent.be

An entire room in the city museum is dedicated to the theft of the Van Eyck panel in 1934. The interior looks like a crime investigation room with scribbled notes on the walls and photographs of the prime suspects. You can listen to recordings of witness statements in English and open 17 wooden drawers containing copies of ransom letters sent by the thief to the Bishop of Ghent.

340 **CLOSER TO VAN EYCK**
closertovaneyck.kikirpa. be

The Getty Foundation has sponsored a unique project to photograph all the panels of the Van Eyck Altarpiece at extremely high resolution. It has also funded a website that allows users to view details of the panel paintings in astonishing microscopic detail.

The 5 most striking paintings in the
MUSEUM OF
FINE ARTS

**MUSEUM
OF FINE ARTS**
Fernand Scribedreef 1
Citadelpark ⑤
+32 (0)9 240 07 00
www.mskgent.be

341 CHRIST CARRYING THE CROSS

Hieronymus Bosch painted this nightmarish vision in about 1515, towards the end of his life. It shows a serene Christ surrounded by a crowd of 16 grotesque faces and one beautiful woman representing Veronica.

342 FAMILY PORTRAIT

Cornelis De Vos captures the quiet contentment of 17th-century Flemish family life in his portrait of a wealthy couple and their four children. The museum website points out that this painting would have cost as much as a modern family car.

343 **PORTRAIT OF A KLEPTOMANIAC**

Théodore Géricault painted ten portraits of mentally ill people in a Paris hospital. The Ghent Museum of Fine Arts owns one of these extremely compassionate 19th-century paintings, showing the troubled face of a kleptomaniac.

344 **PORTRAIT OF MARGUERITE OF MONS**

Théo Van Rysselberghe painted an affectionate portrait of 10-year-old Marguerite Van Mons in the summer of 1886. She is shown wearing a black dress and a silver bracelet that catches the light. Marguerite went on to marry a Brussels lawyer and died in 1919 at the age of 43.

345 **THE GOOD HOUSE**

Gustave De Smet painted this haunting expressionist work in the 1920s. He was living in the village of Sint-Martens-Latem outside Ghent at the time and mainly painted scenes of peasant life. This work shows two men visiting a brothel.

The 5 best places to find
STREET ART

---

346 WERREGARENSTRAAT

Werregarenstraat
Central Ghent ①

Ghent is dotted with creative work by street artists but you have to look hard to find it. The most astonishing street art project is found in a narrow lane at the back of the Novotel where the city created an official graffiti alley in the 1990s. Since then the walls have become an open air gallery of work by many different artists. But most of the art lasts only a few days before it gets overlaid by something else.

347 VERDEDIGINGSTRAAT

Verdedigingstraat
Citadelpark ⑤

The street artist Bué the Warrior sprayed a side wall in Verdedigingstraat in 2009 with a work titled *Sommige Harten Kloppen op 't Straat* (Some hearts beat on the street). His bright cartoon figures can be found in many other locations across the city.

348 SINT-PIETERS-NIEUWSTRAAT

Sint-Pieters-nieuwstraat 194
University Quarter ⑥

The street artists Bué the Warrior and Resto worked together in 2013 to create a striking mural on the side wall of De Salon café in the university quarter. The inspiration comes from soft colourful toys and urban life.

349 TWEEBRUGGEN-STRAAT

Tweebruggenstraat 34
University Quarter ⑥

The city brought in 35 artists in 2012 to create street art on a blank wall outside a Catholic school. The artists were asked to create works on the theme of cycling. The street artist Din Din created an affectionate paste-on drawing of a mother cycling with her six children in a typical Belgian *bakfiets*.

350 ART SCHOOL

Baudelopark
St-Jacobs Quarter ④

Some inspiring street art can be found hidden behind the art school on Ottogracht. Here several walls on the edge of the Baudelopark have been decorated by street artists such as Bué the Warrior.

346 WERREGARENSTRAAT

The 5 most
SECRET INTERIORS

---

351 HOTEL D'HANE-STEENHUYSE

Veldstraat 55
Central Ghent ①

The town house once owned by the d'Hane-Steenhuyse family has one of the finest interiors in Ghent, yet most people walk straight past it. King Louis XVIII of France stayed here for several months after Napoleon forced him to flee from France. The 18th-century building has some magnificent rooms including a glittering ballroom, but it is hard to find a day when it is open.

352 SINT-PIETERSABDIJ REFECTORY

Sint-Pietersplein 9
University Quarter ⑥
+32 (0)9 243 97 30
sintpietersabdijgent.be

Hardly anyone knows about the painted ceiling in the Sint-Pietersabdij. You need to take the Alison audio tour to see this spectacular mediaeval roof decorated with 18th-century scenes from the Old and New Testament. You might be surprised to notice that many of the painted scenes refer to episodes in the Bible involving eating and drinking.

353 DE BIJLOKE

Bijlokekaai 7
Bijloke Quarter ③
+32 (0)9 233 68 78
www.debijloke.be

Here is a stunning venue located in an ancient hospital ward built from grey Tournai stone in 1251-55. The vast interior still has the original oak beamed roof constructed from trees felled in the Ardennes. The interior was restored in 1999 to create an inspiring concert venue with a programme that ranges from classical to jazz.

354 BANK VAN ARBEID

Voldersstraat 1
Central Ghent ①
www.sogent.be

The Bank van Arbeid was built by the socialist party in the 1920s in a grand neo-classical style, but it went bust during the 1934 banking crisis. It is now occupied by the Ghent urban development corporation SoGent and used for temporary exhibitions on town planning. It's worth going inside to wander around the impressive banking hall and take a look inside the former safe room in the basement.

355 HET PAND

Onderbergen 1
Central Ghent ①
ugent.be/het-pand/nl

This ancient Dominican friary is a grim stone building rising out of the water. It was restored by the university to provide lecture rooms as well as tiny monk's cells for university staff. The old refectory is a splendid Gothic space, while the upper cloister has curious stained-glass fragments in display cases. The building contains several unusual museums, including one devoted to Hieronymus Bosch, but you will be lucky to find any of them open.

The 5 most
MYSTERIOUS
SCULPTURES

---

356 THE LITTLE GIRL WITH THE KNITTING NEEDLES

Zilverhof 35
Patershol ②

Only a few people notice the little bronze statue of a girl with knitting needles on the corner of a house in the Patershol. It was created in 1976 by a French artist called Jean-Pierre Clemençon who incorporated some odd symbols including a broken column, a car wheel and a jam jar.

357 NEPTUNE

Sint-Veerleplein
Central Ghent ①

The flamboyant 17th-century baroque gate that once led into the old fish market is surmounted by a splendid figure of Neptune surrounded by seahorses and dolphins. The two naked figures below the sea god represent the rivers that meet in Ghent. The man on the left holding a sail symbolises the Leie, while the woman on the right with a catch of fish stands for the far more important Scheldt.

358 DIVING LADY
Ketelpoort
Central Ghent ①

A bronze statue of a diving woman stands on a balcony overlooking the River Leie. Created by the British artist Ronald Cameron, it was acquired by a local collector. A bronze statue of a diving man stands on the roof of a building on the opposite side of the river.

359 DE MAMMELOKKER
Emile Braunplein/
Botermarkt 17
Central Ghent ①

Look out for the strange carved stone relief above the entrance to a small 18th-century building, formerly a prison, at the foot of the Belfry. Known as De Mammelokker (literally 'the breast suckler'), the sculpture illustrates the old Roman legend in which a man called Cimon was being starved to death in prison when his daughter Pero visited him and fed him from her breast. You can now buy a local beer called Mammelokker.

360 BRUGES-LA-MORTE
Begijnhofdries
Patershol ②

A strange Symbolist figure of a woman was carved by the sculptor George Minne in 1903 to commemorate Georges Rodenbach's 1892 novel *Bruges-la-Morte*. It was originally intended to stand in front of the Begijnhof in Bruges, but the city didn't agree and so Bruges-la-Morte ended up outside the old St.-Elisabeth Begijnhof in Ghent.

The 5 best places to find
STREET ART BY ROA

---

361 THE STORK
Hagelandkaai 39
Dampoort ⑧

The mysterious street artist ROA has painted beautiful works featuring wild animals in London, New York and Paris. But he started out in his home town of Ghent, where several works have survived. One of the most spectacular is a stork on the side wall of a student house near Dampoort station. The bird is painted with one leg raised so that it looks as if it is stepping over a street sign.

362 THE RAVEN
Ketelvest 73
Central Ghent ①

Stand on the bridge over the Ketelvaart canal and you will spot a black raven painted by ROA on a blank wall behind Panos bakery. Here, as always, the artist obtained permission from the building's owner before he started to paint the wall.

363 OUDE BETONFABRIEK
Koopvaardijlaan
Dampoort ⑧

ROA painted a series of animals on the walls of an abandoned cement works in the old docklands. A few animals have survived in this industrial ruin, though most have vanished.

364 FOUR RABBITS
Tempelhof 28
Central Ghent ①

ROA is fond of locations in quiet side streets where no one ever goes. In one hidden corner of Ghent, he has painted four sleeping rabbits on a blank white wall. In London, he painted a huge rabbit on the wall of a recording studio in Hackney. The local council tried to paint it over, but a Facebook campaign saved the work.

365 THE SLEEPING BUFFALO
Kapelaanstraat
Dampoort ⑧

'Ghent is a mellow city where pretty much everything is possible,' ROA once said in an interview. His sleeping animals seem to embody this mellow mood perfectly. This slumbering buffalo is painted on a blank wall belonging to a Turkish wholesale food store in a quiet street near the Sint-Baafs Abbey.

364 **FOUR RABBITS**

The 5 most inspiring
DANCE AND THEATRE COMPANIES

---

366 ONTROEREND GOED
www.ontroerendgoed.be

Alexander Devriendt's collective Ontroerend Goed has been staging powerful experimental productions since they first performed in the Hotsy Totsy bar in 2001. They put on plays that break the rules of theatre and leave often audiences profoundly unsettled. Some say it is not theatre at all, but the company has won numerous awards and performances consistently sell out. The company is now on tour so much of the time that it is hard to find them performing in their home town any more.

367 LES BALLETS C DE LA B
Bijlokekaai 1
Bijloke Quarter ③
+32 (0)9 221 75 01
www.lesballetscdela.be

One of the Europe's most influential dance companies is based in a striking glass building in southern Ghent. Founded by Alain Platel and his sister in 1984, it was ambitiously named Les Ballets Contemporaines de la Belgique. The company has built up a reputation for daring productions, including one involving 65 babies.

368 COMPAGNIE CECILIA

compagnie-cecilia.be

Look out for productions by this exciting Ghent theatre company based in the old port area. Founded in 2006 by Arne Sierens and Johan Heldenbergh, Compagnie Cecilia presents energetic performances that combine music, circus and slapstick. The acclaimed film *The Broken Circle Breakdown* was based on a 2008 play staged by the company.

369 NTGENT

Sint-Baafsplein 17
Central Ghent ①
+32 (0)9 225 01 01
www.ntgent.be

This theatre company puts on plays and performances in a striking 1899 Flemish renaissance building. NTGent specialises in edgy contemporary theatre in Dutch, but its programme also features opera, concerts, poetry readings and kids' performances.

370 LOD

www.lod.be

This young Ghent company creates daring operas and musical theatre productions that combine contemporary music, theatre, visual art and philosophy. The Ghent city composer is often involved in LOD productions.

The 5 best independent
ART GALLERIES

---

371 **KIOSK**
Louis Pasteurlaan 2
Bijloke Quarter ③
+32 (0)9 267 01 68
www.kioskgallery.be

This gallery has been located since 2010 in a former anatomy theatre inside the old Bijloke hospital. You may spend some time wandering through the warren of former hospital corridors before you find the place. Four shows a year are held in the striking Neo-Gothic interior.

372 **THESE THINGS TAKE TIME**
Nederkouter 36
Bijloke Quarter ③
+32 (0)474 75 82 74
thesethingstaketime.be

A disused shop on a busy street in the student quarter has been turned into a small art space with a radical manifesto. The founder Matthias Yzebaert is still working out what he wants to do with his gallery, but he seems to be moving in the direction of art happenings and random parties.

373 **CROXHAPOX**
Lucas Munichstraat 76
Dampoort ⑧
+32 (0)471 44 13 62
croxhapox.org

It doesn't want to be a gallery. It definitely doesn't want to sell art. But Croxhapox has built up a solid reputation for showing exciting experimental art since it opened in 1990. Its programme includes music, film and poetry, as well as some edgy art.

374 FLINXO

Ottogracht 38
St-Jacobs Quarter ④
+32 (0)474 32 64 58
flinxo.com

This small photographers' gallery puts on interesting and sometimes provocative exhibitions by Belgian and international photographers. Look out for the huge photograph sometimes hung from the front of the building to advertise the latest show.

375 A&GALLERY

Schepenhuisstraat 17
Central Ghent ①
www.angels-ghosts.com

Ben van Alboom and Wouter Van Vaerenbergh opened this gallery just behind the town hall in 2011. They exhibit works by edgy contemporary artists, along with their own rock music photography project Angels & Ghosts.

373 CROXHAPOX

The 5 strangest
ART INSTALLATIONS

---

376 MONUMENT
Sint-Pietersplein
University Quarter ⑥

This mural is not too easy to find unless you know where to look. It was created in 2011 by the artist Anouk De Clercq on the side wall of a staircase leading down to an underground car park. Intended to serve as a monument to student life, the work represents shelves of books in Ghent university library. But the strangest part goes unnoticed by most people. You have to approach the work to hear the faint sounds recorded by the artist to represent students whispering in the library.

377 AI NATI OGGI
Sint-Veerleplein
Central Ghent ①

The lamp-posts on Sint-Veerleplein have been programmed to flicker every time a child is born in a Ghent maternity ward. The Italian artist Alberto Garutti created this installation during the TRACK art event in 2012. He called it *Ai Nati Oggi* (to those born today), but you may have to wait a long time for a birth in this small town.

378 MUSEUM GRAVEYARD
Louis Van Houtte-
dreef
Citadelpark ⑤

The Ghent artist Leo Copers created a haunting mock cemetery in 2012 for the art event TRACK. Dotted among the old trees are 111 gravestones carved with the names of famous art museums. The fake memorials were left standing in the park after the art event ended, but they might not stay here forever.

379 THE BIG VASE
Jan Breydelstraat 5
Central Ghent ①
+32 (0)9 267 99 99
designmuseumgent.be

An enormous green vase stands in the inner courtyard of the Design Museum. The nine-metre-high object was designed in 1999 by the Italian architect Andrea Branzi.

380 THE EXTERMINATING ANGEL
Augustijnenkaai
Patershol ②

An avenging angel wearing a gas mask stands on top of a globe in the courtyard of the Augustine Monastery. This eerie work was made by the Brussels sculptor Tom Frantzen for a 2013 exhibition of his work held in the former monastery.

378 MUSEUM GRAVEYARD

STUDIO MIE

20 PLACES TO SLEEP

The 5 most
STYLISH B&BS

381 LOGID'ENRI

Brabantdam 201
Central Ghent ①
+32 (0)9 225 35 77
www.logidenri.be

Interior architect Didier Michiels and his wife have created a sublime B&B in a white town house. The 19th-century building has been decorated in a beautiful contemporary style to create a 5-room B&B with appealing touches such as teak floors and designer chairs.

382 ENGELEN AAN DE WATERKANT

Ter Platen 30
University Quarter ⑥
+32 (0)476 40 25 23
www.engelenaande
waterkant.be

Interior designer Ann Willems runs a B&B in a handsome 19th-century house on the waterfront. The two rooms are beautifully decorated with white furniture and crisp bed linen. The room on the first floor also has a balcony with a table and two chairs.

383 DE WATERZOOI

Sint-Veerleplein 2
Central Ghent ①
+32 (0)9 330 77 21
www.dewaterzooi.be

Kay and Christian Delens have lovingly restored a 17th-century house facing the Gravensteen to create a gorgeous B&B. The two suites are decorated in a Flemish country house style with big white sofas, comfortable beds, rustic stairs and blazing fires.

384 CHAMBRE PLUS

Hoogpoort 31
Central Ghent ①
+32 (0)9 225 37 75
www.chambreplus.be

Mia Ackaert is a cook and Hendrik Mesuere is a chocolatier. Together they have created a beautiful B&B in an 18th-century town house in the heart of the old town. The three rooms are richly decorated in African Colonial style. The attic room has the added attraction of a jacuzzi in a bathroom with a roof that opens to the stars in fine weather.

385 GEERTJE HENCKENS

Zwartezustersstraat 3
Central Ghent ①
+32 (0)9 224 34 05
www.slapen-in-gent.be

Geertje Henckens runs a friendly B&B in a former monastery in the centre of Ghent. The three rooms are comfortable, but rather simple. You can sit outside in the summer in the leafy back garden and eat breakfast at a long wooden table. This is the perfect address for a young couple on a modest budget.

381 LOGID'ENRI

The 5 most
ROMANTIC PLACES
to spend the night

386 HÔTEL VERHAEGEN

Oude Houtlei 110
Central Ghent ①
+32 (0)9 265 07 60
www.neooselonneo.be

This is a sublime romantic hideaway located in a white rococo town house with a formal garden at the back. The owners have furnished the five bedrooms with a creative mixture of 18th-century antiques and contemporary objects. Breakfast is served in a charming rococo salon with a blazing fire in winter.

387 HARMONY

Kraanlei 37
Central Ghent ①
+32 (0)9 324 26 80
www.hotel-harmony.be

This beautiful family-run hotel has spacious bedrooms and luxurious bathrooms. The waterfront location in the heart of the city is perfect for exploring the old city.

388 HANCELOT

Vijfwindgaten-
straat 19
University Quarter ⑥
+32 (0)9 234 35 45
www.hancelot.be

This charming hotel occupies a lovingly-restored town house built for a Belgian baron in the 1840s. The rooms have a period grandeur with creaking wooden floors, high ceilings and crystal chandeliers. The hotel is located in a quiet residential quarter not too far from the old centre.

389 SANDTON GRAND HOTEL REYLOF

Hoogstraat 36
Central Ghent ⓘ
+32 (0)9 235 40 70
www.sandton.eu/gent

This luxurious hotel occupies a white 18th-century mansion once owned by a baron. The main rooms are grand and elegant, with parquet floors, a sweeping staircase and an open fire. The former coach house where the baron once kept his horses now contains a small pool and sauna.

390 ERASMUS

Poel 25
Central Ghent ⓘ
+32 (0)9 224 21 95
www.erasmushotel.be

Here is a fine old-fashioned hotel located in a town house that dates from the 16th century. Everything looks old, even the website. Some might find the bedrooms a bit dark and dated, but others will love the atmosphere in an old building that has been around for centuries.

388 HANCELOT

The 5 best
CHEAP LODGINGS

391 ONDERBERGEN

Onderbergen 69
Central Ghent ①
+32 (0)9 223 62 00
hotelonderbergen.be

This is a comfortable hotel with spacious rooms located in a historic old town building. It is hard to find anywhere cheaper to stay in central Ghent, especially if you have children. The staff are exceptionally friendly, but maybe you can skip the breakfast served in the Irish pub next door and eat in one of the cool local coffee bars.

392 HOSTEL UPPELINK

Sint-Michielsplein 21
Central Ghent ①
+32 (0)9 279 44 77
hosteluppelink.com

This beautiful new hostel opened recently in an ancient stone building dating from 1200. Located on the Graslei canal, it has a rugged interior with bare brick walls, ancient wood beams and stunning views of the old city. It's the perfect place for a single traveller or a student just landed in Ghent. The owners are exceptionally friendly and the bar is a relaxed spot to make new friends.

393 BACKSTAY HOSTEL

Sint-Pietersnieuw-
straat 128
University Quarter ⑥
+32 (0)9 395 96 60
backstayhostels.com

This new hotel opened in 2014 in a striking Art Deco building. The socialist newspaper Vooruit was edited here until it closed down in the 1980s. The building has been carefully restored and modernised to provide cheap dorm accommodation and inexpensive double rooms in the heart of the university district.

394 PLACE 2 STAY

Penitentenstraat 33
St-Jacobs Quarter ④
+32 (0)486 38 42 58
place2stayinghent.be

Nele and Willem rent out smart and spacious apartments in an interesting neighbourhood dotted with unusual antique shops and little jazz bars. The apartments have everything you need, including comfortable beds and well-stocked kitchens, though the interior design is a little bland. You may have to phone Nele when you arrive as she is not always around, and you have to pay cash.

395 APARTHOTEL CASTELNOU

Kasteellaan 51
University Quarter ⑥
+32 (0)9 235 04 11
www.castelnou.be

A modern apartment hotel decorated in a rather sober style. But you get a generous sitting area, a separate kitchen with an espresso machine and a spacious bathroom. You are on the edge of the city here with very few restaurants in the neighbourhood, but a pleasant 20-minute canalside walk gets you into the centre.

The 5 most
UNUSUAL PLACES TO STAY

---

396 STUDIOMIE

Bomastraat 20
Dampoort ⑧
+32 (0)497 43 26 42
www.studiomie.be

Mieke De Maeyer has created a curious B&B inside a shipping container perched high above an industrial space. The interior is designed in a playful contemporary style with plywood walls, a tiny shower and a folding ladder up to the bedroom. We liked the little handwritten notes, the jewellery to borrow, the generous breakfast and the notebook full of Mieke's personal tips.

397 SNOOZ INN

Ham 89
Dampoort ⑧
+32 (0)496 24 14 26
www.snoozinn.be

Here is a friendly new B&B located in an old printing works. It lies a ten-minute walk from the centre in a quiet urban neighbourhood. The bedrooms are designed in a cool minimalist style with a home cinema and a blue glowing shower cabin bang in the middle of the room.

398 SHELTER 7

Bennesteeg 7
Central Ghent ①
+32 (0)498 85 62 39
www.shelter7.be

This is a gorgeous urban retreat on three floors hidden away above Blanco bike store. Created by Belgian designer Raymond Jacquemyns, it has a living room with an open fire on one floor, a bathroom and terrace above and a bedroom on the top floor. The interior is dotted with vintage design objects and stacks of magazines to read by the fire.

399 B3

Zuidkaai 43
Western Ghent
+32 (0)477 54 00 03

The owners of the Bed and Breakfast Boat have turned a handsome old river barge into a quirky B&B where you wake to the sound of ducks. Moored on a quiet canal near the old town, B3 has two comfortable rooms, including a stylish captain's cabin with its own entrance and sitting room. A generous breakfast is brought to your room in a wicker basket and in the summer you can sit out on the deck.

400 EXPO 13

Prinses
Clementinalaan 13
Station Quarter ⑦
+32 (0)475 28 93 85
www.expo13.be

This handsome B&B occupies a 19th-century town house near Sint-Pieters-station. The five rooms have bare wooden floors, old marble fireplaces and vintage bathtubs. The owners are very welcoming and provide a generous breakfast. Room 5, tucked below the attic, is the perfect romantic hideaway.

GHENT BY NIGHT

50 ACTIVITIES
FOR WEEKENDS

———

The 5 best
URBAN WALKS

---

401 ACHTERVISSERIJ
Achtervisserij
Dampoort ⑧

One of the best waterfront walks in Ghent begins at Dampoort station and follows the tree-lined quay Schoolkaai to reach the River Leie. The route then continues down a quiet stretch of waterfront until the river splits. Here you can follow the overgrown towpath Achtervisserij to discover a forgotten corner of Ghent where locals paddle in canoes past factory walls sprayed with graffiti by Bué the Warrior.

402 LEIE WATERFRONT
Bijlokekaai
Bijloke Quarter ③

One of the best urban walks in Europe follows the quiet, overgrown quay Bijlokekaai, with strange fin-de-siècle university buildings on one side and steep gardens and old tea houses on the opposite bank. The walk continues along Lindenlei, then crosses over to the other bank at the start of Predikherenlei. Here you see the ancient stone monastery Het Pand on the opposite bank before passing under the Sint-Michielsbrug to emerge on the beautiful Graslei waterfront.

403 GHENT AFTER DARK

Sint-Michielsbrug
Central Ghent ①
www.gentverlicht.be

Ghent is an exceptionally atmospheric city after dark because of dramatic new lighting installed in 1998. Start a night walk on Sint-Michielsbrug and follow the waterfront north to the Vrijdagmarkt. Then head east to the streets around the Sint-Jacobskerk.

404 ART NOUVEAU WALK

Citadelpark ⑤

A one-hour walk through the streets around the Citadelpark takes you past some of Ghent's most beautiful Art Nouveau houses. Begin at Sint-Pietersstation and walk down Prinses Clementinalaan to see the flamboyant Art Nouveau houses decorated with ironwork and painted tiles. Then walk down Parklaan, Fortlaan and Kunstlaan.

405 ARCHITECTURE WALK

Muinkkaai
University Quarter ⑥

Some of the most striking architecture in Ghent can be seen if you walk down the narrow towpath that runs along Muinkkaai. Start at the north end, near Woodrow Wilsonplein, and you will see the East Flanders Chamber of Commerce, the back of the 1913 Vooruit building and several university buildings, including the brutalist concrete Faculty of Economics from the 1970s and the new Faculty of Economics Building designed by Stéphane Beel. Then you come to the baroque Sint-Pieters Abbey, followed by the Artevelde College built just beyond the bridge by the architects Crépain-Binst.

The 5 best ways to
GET FIT

---

406 BOURGOYEN WALKING TRAILS

Driepikkelstraat 32
Suburbs

The Bourgoyen-Ossemeersen nature reserve is a fascinating wild area on the edge of town with water meadows, tree-lined trails and woodlands. The fields are flooded for much of the winter but the raised paths remain accessible. You can walk or jog along marked trails or just sit in wooden hides watching rare migrating birds.

407 VAN EYCK POOL

Veermanplein 1
Dampoort ⑧
+32 (0)9 235 27 40
www.gent.be

The most spectacular public pool in Ghent dates back to 1886. It was modernised in the 1930s in Art Deco style and restored in 2001. The original entrance at the front was replaced by a bright new entrance at the back of the building and a modern café was added overlooking the pool.

408 GHENT TO BRUGES CYCLE ROUTE

www.fietsroute.org

You can cycle from Ghent to Bruges and back using old canal towpaths along most of the 100-kilometre route. The shortest route is to follow the 45-km Ghent to Bruges canal, but you can take a slightly longer route back to Ghent that follows towpaths along Damme canal, the Schipdonkkanaal and the Lievekanaal. Book a night in Bruges to make a perfect weekend.

409 WATERSPORTBAAN RUNNING TRAIL

Verenigde Natieslaan
Bijloke Quarter ③

Runners head out to the running trail around the Watersportbaan for some serious training. The artificial waterway was created in 1955 for the European rowing championships and is still used for rowing. It is surrounded by a soft running track that is just 33 metres short of five kilometres. Complete the circuit eight times and you have run a marathon, or almost.

410 ESCAPE FITNESS

Sint-Pieters-
nieuwstraat 132
University Quarter ⑥
+32 (0)9 224 27 37
www.escapefitness.be

Our favourite gym is located at the top of an abandoned office building opposite Vooruit. We like the relaxed atmosphere, the friendly staff and the people of all ages who come here. And after climbing six flights of stairs to reach the fitness hall, you have almost done a complete workout.

The 5 most inspiring places to
PARTY AFTER DARK

---

411 WHITE CAT

Drongenhof 40
Patershol ②
+32 (0)496 18 91 89
www.whitecat.be

This lounge bar is hidden away in a 14th-century cellar in the Patershol. Look for the little cat sculpture above a narrow alleyway. The interior is decorated with 1970s furniture, pink walls and an illuminated fish tank. It can get uncomfortably hot down here as people dance and drink cocktails into the late hours.

412 CLUB 69

Oude Beestenmarkt 5
St-Jacobs Quarter ④
www.club-69.be

Look for the building with the colourful stripes. That is Club 69. It opened in 2011 for people over 21 who want to dance to rock and indie music. A menu at the door lists coming events, while the interior is lit with purple and blue lights to create a relaxed retro mood.

413 CHARLATAN

Vlasmarkt 6
St-Jacobs Quarter ④
+32 (0)9 224 24 57
www.charlatan.be

It may look like an ordinary bar when you step inside, but Charlatan is one of the best places in town to discover new bands. It is surprisingly large inside with a café, dance room and concert hall under one roof. For the past 25 years, this place has hosted every genre of music, along with comedy evenings and gay parties on Sundays. The one problem is that it can get impossibly crowded.

414 DECADANCE

Overpoortstraat 76
University Quarter ⑥
+32 (0)9 329 00 54
www.decadance.be

The hardcore party crowd heads to this underground music club in the student quarter when other places have closed down. The DJs play techno tunes deep into the night in three rooms packed with students on the dance floor.

415 CULTURE CLUB

Afrikalaan 174
Docks Quarter
+32 (0)9 233 09 46
www.cultureclub.be

In 2007 the British style magazine The Face described this docklands venue as the hippest place in Europe. But that was then. Some say Culture Club has lost its edge. But students still flock to the wild parties held out in the depths of the port area.

The 5 best
OFFBEAT TOURS

---

416 VIADAGIO
www.viadagio.be

Viadagio runs ecological boat tours that don't harm the environment or annoy local residents. They use beautiful wooden punts that are hand-crafted in Bangladesh to take you on a silent tour of the city's waterways. Boat tours have to be booked for groups of at least six people. The ideal departure time is around dusk on a warm summer evening.

417 MAX MOBIEL
Stadshal
Emile Braunplein
Central Ghent ①
+32 (0)490 45 27 13
www.max-mobiel.be

Ghent is one of the world's great cycling cities. It has endless dedicated cycle routes and an extensive network of bridges and tunnels to separate bikes from cars. But it's not that easy to rent a bike for a few hours. There are plans to introduce a city bike scheme in 2015, but until then you have to contact Max Mobiel to arrange a bike rental. You book online and pick up the sturdy red bike at one of the main railway stations, or in the underground bike park below the Stadshal.

418 MINERVA BOAT COMPANY

Coupure Rechts 2a
Bijloke Quarter ③
+32 (0)9 233 79 17
www.minervaboten.be

You can spend a summer day exploring the waterways of Ghent on your own little motor boat. The boat can be picked up at a small harbour office near the Kouter for a little trip of a couple of hours, or a full day messing around on the River Leie. The helpful staff tell you everything you need to know about navigating the local waterways.

419 CITY RUNNING GHENT

+32 (0)485 32 44 20
www.readytogo.be

Wim Van De Putte organises running tours around Ghent for people who want to see the city while keeping fit. A brisk one-hour tour starts at the Marriott Hotel and takes in sights like the Gravensteen and the Vooruit. He also organises running tours after dark.

420 TRAM 1

Koningin
Maria Hendrikaplein
Station Quarter ⑦
www.delijn.be

The cheapest way to see the sights is to hop on tram 1. It takes you right through the centre of Ghent, down narrow streets lined with stylish shops, across the busy Korenmarkt and around the grey stone walls of the Gravensteen. Pick up the tram at Sint-Pietersstation.

The 5 most authentic
FESTIVALS

---

421 GENTSE FEESTEN
www.gentsefeesten.be

It started out in 1969 as a small festival with a few local bands on a makeshift stage. Now the Gentse Feesten is the biggest street festival in Europe, attracting more than two million revellers. People come for the music, the beer, but most of all for the wild atmosphere that lasts ten days and nights, beginning on the Saturday before the 21 July Belgian national holiday.

422 ODEGAND
www.odegand.be

A magical festival of classical music is held in the late summer in various venues along the canals. Small ensembles and soloists perform for 45 minutes in unexpected locations. The audiences move around by canal boat, sampling an eclectic programme of classical, jazz, fado and techno. The festival ends with a free waterfront concert on the Graslei.

423 PRINSENHOF-FEESTEN

users.telenet.be/dekenij/10-ProgFEESTEN.html

This friendly street festival takes place over one weekend in September in the Prinsenhof neighbourhood, where a 15th-century palace once stood. Its attractions include a flea market, a procession through the old quarter, jazz bands and endless street food.

424 GHENT SIX DAYS

Citadelpark ⑤

www.lottozesdaagse.be

This tough cycling race has been held every winter since 1922 in the Kuipke velodrome in the Citadelpark. Cycling fans flock here on damp November nights to cheer on professional cyclists who complete thousands of laps over six days. By the end, the air is thick with the smell of beer, hamburgers and damp sweat.

425 GHENT LIGHT FESTIVAL

www.lichtfestivalgent.be

Ghent organises a light festival every three years in the depths of winter. Skilled artists and designers create extraordinary light effects including entire buildings made out of coloured light bulbs. The next festival happens in January 2018.

The 5 uncommon places seen from
TRAM 4

---

426 KONING ALBERTLAAN 97
Koning Albertlaan 97
Station Quarter ⑦

Most people take tram 1 to get from the station to the city centre. But there is a lot more to see if you pick up tram 4 outside the main station heading in the direction Moscou. Sit on the left side if you can for the best view. Not long after leaving the station, the tram passes a series of grand Art Deco houses on the gently curving Koning Albertlaan, including a striking modernist building with ornate ironwork at No. 97.

427 RABOT
Rabot stop
Patershol ②

The route of tram 4 runs close to the grey stone towers of the last surviving city gate. Known as *Het Rabot*, this rugged watergate was built over the River Lieve in 1491 to control boats entering the city.

428 DE NIEUWE MOLENS
Biervlietstraat stop
Northern Ghent

After passing Rabot, tram 4 runs past new law courts designed by Stéphane Beel. Beyond lies a complex of grain silos called *De Nieuwe Molens* where the city is currently constructing some inspiring new apartment buildings.

429 SAS VAN GENT

Muidebrug stop
Northern Ghent

Tram 4 passes close to the old harbour quarter Sas van Gent, which is linked to the North Sea by a canal dug in 1563 and widened in the 1820s. The harbour is still used by inland barges.

430 RIHERA

Sleepstraat 216
Northern Ghent

Look out for the bow of a canal barge named Rihera in the square in front of the Heilige-Kerstkerk. It was put there as a reminder of the maritime history of this quarter. Inside the church are some remarkable paintings as well as a replica barge built by local craftsmen.

The 5 fun things to
DO WITH KIDS

---

431 BLAARMEERSEN
Zuiderlaan 5
Suburbs
www.blaarmeersen.be

You can spend a whole day with kids at a big lake called Blaarmeersen on the edge of the city. The lake is bordered by sandy beaches, adventure playgrounds and woods, along with a skate park, mini golf and pedal boats for rent. There are several cafés around the lakeside, including the relaxed Le Beach House where kids can run wild in an indoor playground.

432 DOK STRAND
Koopvaardijlaan
Dampoort ⑧
www.dokgent.be

An area of abandoned dockland near the Dampoort is transformed every year into a sandy city beach with paddling pools, deck chairs and smouldering barbeques. It's a great place to take your kids on a Sunday to experience the cool, relaxed mood of Ghent at its best. But the area is slowly being redeveloped for housing and the beach may not last here many more years.

433 KINA

Sint-Pietersplein 14
University Quarter ⑥
+32 (0)9 244 73 73
dewereldvankina.be

It used to be called the School Museum, but that sounded a bit dull, so it was renamed *De wereld van Kina* (The world of Kina). Established in 1924 as a museum of natural history, it now occupies a baroque wing of the Sint-Pieters abbey. Some of the exhibits might seem old-fashioned, like the fossil collection and the stuffed animals in glass cases, but there are also fun interactive games and an impressive scale model of Ghent in the 16th century.

434 DE BOOTJES VAN GENT

Korenlei 4A
Central Ghent ①
+32 (0)9 229 17 16
debootjesvangent.be

Children are likely to enjoy taking a boat tour on the Ghent canals starting at the little green cabin on the Korenlei waterfront. The enthusiastic guides provide a lively commentary during the 40-minute tour as you are steered past the Gravensteen castle and the Rabot city gate.

435 DE WERELD VAN KINA: DE TUIN

Berouw 55
Northern Ghent
+32 (0)9 225 05 42
dewereldvankina.be

The old entrance to the School Museum is still standing in a quiet street in northern Ghent, although the museum has moved elsewhere. But go through the gate and you will discover a forgotten botanical garden designed to appeal to small children. You can roam around the garden finding out about bees and spiders, then head to the café for a hot chocolate.

The 5 best
SMALL CINEMAS

436 STUDIO SKOOP

Sint-Annaplein 63
University Quarter ⑥
+32 (0)9 225 08 45
www.studioskoop.be

This inspiring filmhouse has been screening movies in five small rooms since 1970. It is located in a handsome building originally occupied by the union of veterans of the First World War and used during the Second World War as a brothel for German officers. The programme mainly features thoughtful alternative films.

437 SPHINX

Sint-Michielshelling 3
Central Ghent ①
+32 (0)9 225 60 86
www.sphinx-cinema.be

They started screening films in this cinema next to the Sint-Michielsbrug in 1912. Sphinx now has five rooms where they show a varied programme of hit movies and award-winning films from international festivals. We love the small screening room on the top floor (Sphinx 4) which has just 45 seats.

438 KASK

Godhuizenlaan 4
Bijloke Quarter ③
+32 (0)9 267 01 09
www.kaskcinema.be

This small art cinema located within the old Bijloke hospital is run by the School of Arts. The audience is mainly made up of students from the film course, who come here to watch experimental movies that are not screened anywhere else.

439 CINE PALACE

Minnemeers 9
St-Jacobs Quarter ④
+32 (0)9 269 87 50
www.miat.gent.be

You really would not expect to find an old Art Deco cinema on the fourth floor of a museum of industrial archaeology. But there it is. The interior has been lovingly recreated, right down to the bare wood floor, red velvet seats and antique neon sign giving the ticket price as four francs. The cinema screens classic arthouse films on old projectors every second Sunday at 10.15 and 14.30.

440 OFFOFF

Begijnhof ter Hoye
Lange Violette-
straat 237
University Quarter ⑥
+32 (0)9 335 31 83
www.offoff.be

This tiny non-profit art cinema is located in one of the old Begijnhof houses. It describes itself as a 'screening and research platform for experimental film.' They show obscure old films that have vanished without trace along with new productions by directors who are pushing the boundaries of cinema.

439 CINE PALACE

The 5 most
IMPORTANT DATES
in Ghent's history

---

441 24 FEBRUARY 1540

Bachtenwalle
Patershol ②

On this day, Charles V marked his 40th birthday by punishing leading city officials who had refused to pay a new tax. They were ordered to walk barefoot through the city wearing hangman's nooses around their necks. A modern statue of a *Stroppendrager* (Noose Wearer) stands facing the old gate that once led into the Prinsenhof.

442 26 APRIL 1913

Station Quarter ⑦

Ghent hosted an ambitious World Fair that opened on 26 April 1913 on an extensive site in southern Ghent. The Greek chocolate maker Leonidas had opened a tea room in Ghent earlier in the year and went on to win a gold medal at the World Fair for his chocolates.

443 **11 APRIL 1934**

Sint-Baafsplein
Central Ghent ①

On this morning, an official in Ghent Cathedral discovered that two panels had been stolen from the Van Eyck Altarpiece. One panel was later recovered in a Brussels railway station, but the other remains missing, despite countless attempts to find it.

444 **16 NOVEMBER 1949**

Veerleplein 11
Central Ghent ①
+32 (0)9 267 14 66
gravensteengent.be

On this day, the Gravensteen was stormed by 136 Ghent students protesting at a rise in the price of beer. They locked themselves inside the ancient castle walls and hurled rotten fruit from the battlements as the police tried to expel them. The fire brigade eventually recaptured the castle using long ladders. The Siege of the Gravensteen is celebrated every year on 16 November with a noisy student procession.

445 **21 JUNE 1986**

+32 (0)9 240 76 01
www.smak.be

In the summer of 1986, the art museum director Jan Hoet invited 51 contemporary artists to create works to be exhibited in private homes across the city. The event, which was called *Chambres d'Amis* (Guest Rooms), included artists such as Daniel Buren and Joseph Beuys. A few of the works have survived in various locations.

The 5 best
PLACES NEAR GHENT
to visit

446 PORT OF GHENT

Rigakaai
Ghent port
+32 (0)9 251 05 50
www.havengent.be

Hardly anyone ever visits the port to the north of Ghent. But it can easily be done by booking a place on one of the free boat tours organised by the port every Saturday afternoon. During the two-hour cruise, you can stand out on the deck looking at the industrial landscape, or sit down below in the café with a local beer. Booking can be done online.

447 AFSNEE

Afsnee
Suburbs

Here is a beautiful village on a bend in the River Leie with an ancient Romanesque church down by the water and a ferryman who takes cyclists and ramblers across the river in a little punt (on summer days at least). You can stop for a beer in the village in a friendly café called Sfinx or walk down the river bank to an old waterside bar called Oude Drie Leien.

448 OOIDONK CASTLE
Ooidonkdreef
Deinze
+32 (0)9 282 35 70
www.ooidonk.be

Ooidonk Castle stands in quiet watery meadows near the River Leie. It is a spectacular Flemish renaissance building with round turrets and a moat. You can visit the castle and its gardens by ringing the caretaker's bell at the entrance. The former coach house near the entrance has been turned into a rustic restaurant where you can eat a quick lunch or a three-course meal.

449 'T OUD SASHUIS
Hellestraat 20
Astene

You can hike from Ooidonk along the Ooidonk wandelroute, a walking trail that takes you along the meandering River Leie. You pass close to 't Oud Sashuis, a friendly little Flemish bar in an old lock-keeper's house. The interior is crammed with shipping mementoes, old photographs and dried sausages hanging on strings, while French chanson plays in the background.

450 DEURLE
Deurle
Sint-Martens-Latem

Deurle is a beautiful old village on a bend in the River Leie where several Flemish artists settled in the early 20th century. The village is dotted with small museums in former artist's houses as well as romantic hotels and rustic restaurants.

GRASLEI

50 RANDOM FACTS AND URBAN DETAILS

The 5 most intriguing possible
HIDING PLACES
of the stolen Van Eyck

---

451 CATHEDRAL CRYPT
Sint-Baafsplein
Central Ghent ①

There are countless theories about the hiding place of the stolen Just Judges panel, which was wrenched from the Ghent Altarpiece in 1934 and never recovered. One theory is that it is hidden in the Cathedral, perhaps in one of the dark spaces in the Crypt.

452 GEERAARD DE DUIVELSTEEN
Geraard de Duivel-straat 1
Central Ghent ①

One year after the theft, a Flemish newspaper ran a story that the panel was hidden in a 'public building near the Cathedral'. This led the police to search the ancient stone fortress known as Geeraard the Devil's Castle. They carried out an investigation, but found no trace of the panel in the somber mediaeval building.

453 VAN EYCK HOUSE

Koestraat 50
Central Ghent ①

A Flemish writer claimed to have discovered a secret code that indicated the missing panel was hidden in a 19th-century corner house on Koestraat. The house is believed to be the site of the building where the Ghent Altarpiece was painted by Jan and Hubert van Eyck (whose heads can be seen on the façade). But nothing was found when the building was searched in 1991.

454 SINT-JANSVEST GARAGE

Sint-Jansvest 38
Central Ghent ①

An amateur detective came up with a theory in 2008 that the missing panel was hidden in an old garage down a back street near the Ketelvest canal. The police carried out a careful search but came up with nothing.

455 KOMIJNSTRAAT 1

Komijnstraat 1
Central Ghent ①

Art experts came from Brussels to search a house in central Ghent in 1978. They had found out that it was once occupied by a relative of the stockbroker Arsène Goedertier, who was a prime suspect in the investigation. But nothing was found inside the house.

The 5 most famous people
BORN IN GHENT

---

456 JOHN OF GAUNT

Voorhoutkaai 43
Dampoort ⑧
+32 (0)9 243 97 30
burenvandeabdij.be

The third son of Edward III of England was born in Ghent in 1340. His mother Queen Philippa gave birth in the abbey of Sint-Baafs while Edward III was away fighting a war. John of Gaunt makes a famous dying speech in Shakespeare's Richard II in which he praised England as 'This blessed plot, this earth, this realm, this England.'

457 EMPEROR CHARLES V

Prinsenhofplein
Patershol ②

On 24 February 1500, Joanna of Castile gave birth to a son in the Prinsenhof in Ghent. The boy grew up to become Emperor Charles V, who ruled over the Low Countries, Spain and Portugal. He became deeply unpopular in Ghent after he punished the city for refusing to pay a tax. But a statue of Charles V was finally put up in 1966 in a little square where the Prinsenhof once stood.

458 LIEVEN BAUWENS

Reep
Central Ghent ①

In 1899, the Ghent industrialist Lieven Bauwens smuggled parts of a Spinning Jenny out of Manchester hidden among sacks of coffee. He was accused by Britain of industrial espionage and sentenced to death. But Bauwens became a local hero in Ghent where he set up the first cotton factory in an abandoned monastery in 1800. A statue was put up in his honour in 1885.

459 LEO BAEKELAND

The world's first synthetic material was invented by the chemist Leo Baekeland, who was born in Ghent in 1863. His father was a cobbler and his mother worked as a maid. Leo moved to America and made his name in 1909 with the invention he called Bakelite. This hard, versatile plastic was used extensively in the manufacture of radios, telephones and televisions. Baekeland is celebrated in America as the founder of the plastics industry, but he remains almost forgotten in Ghent.

460 BRADLEY WIGGINS

Gasmeterlaan
Patershol ②

The British cyclist and Olympic champion Bradley Wiggins was born in an apartment in a poor district of northern Ghent in 1980. His father Gary was an Australian professional cyclist who raced in Belgium. Wiggins left Belgium when he was three.

The 5 most
INSPIRING URBAN
INITIATIVES

---

461 PARNASSUS

Oude Houtlei 122
Central Ghent ①
+32 (0)9 223 23 41
www.parnassus.be

A beautiful baroque church that once belonged to the Franciscans has been turned into a social restaurant and concert hall. You can eat a healthy and inexpensive lunch amid the beautiful baroque confessionals and Catholic statues.

462 CITY SHEEP

Coupure &
Bijloke-complex
Bijloke Quarter ③

The city keeps a small flock of some 30 sheep to graze on canal banks and small parks. The sheep can sometimes be spotted on the banks of the Coupure canal or in the grounds of the Bijloke complex, accompanied by the city's shepherd and sheepdog.

463 VISTUIN

Achtervisserij
Dampoort ⑧

Joksie Biesemans created her strange waterfront garden in 2012 using junk she had fished out of the Ghent waterways while paddling through the city in her canoe. Her *Vistuin* (Fish Garden) has plants growing in rusted tin cans, old slippers, plastic tubes, a toilet bowl and even a television that someone dumped.

464 VEGGIE DAY
donderdagveggiedag.be

Ghent has always been a progressive little town. It proved the point in 2009 by launching a weekly 'veggie Thursday' to persuade people to take a day off from eating meat. The local schools and municipal canteens now enthusiastically support the scheme.

465 GREEN BASTARDS GARDEN
Sint-Pieters-
nieuwstraat 23
University Quarter ⑥
vooruit.be

A team of radical gardeners has created a vertical garden on the side wall of the Vooruit cultural centre. They use recycled bicycle wheels and hospital drip bags to nurture vegetables and herbs that are no longer grown commercially. Their big idea is to cultivate seeds that can be used by locals to grow their own vegetables.

461 PARNASSUS

The 5 most watchable
GHENT FILMS

---

466 ROMEO.JULIET

A bizarre film version of Romeo and Juliet was partly shot in Ghent in 1990 using several hundred cats. Directed by Armando Acosta, it features John Hurt improbably playing a Venetian bag lady. The film was first screened in Brussels, but it is now almost impossible to find a copy.

467 STEVE + SKY

The Flemish director Felix Van Groeningen set his strange 2004 film on the sex strip that runs along the Kortrijksesteenweg between Ghent and Kortrijk. The film charts the relationship between Steve, who is trying to go straight after coming out of jail, and Sky, a dancer in a night club. It is filmed mostly at night as Steve cruises the strip in search of motorbikes to steal, passing gaudy sex bars, brightly-lit petrol stations and Chinese restaurants. The soundtrack is by the Ghent band Soulwax.

468 **BROKEN CIRCLE BREAKDOWN**

One of the most successful Belgian films ever made, Felix van Groeningen's 2012 *Broken Circle Breakdown* was filmed in unknown corners of Ghent against a background of bluegrass music. It tells the story of a bearded banjo player and a woman covered in tattoos whose lives are shattered when their young daughter dies of cancer. Originally a play by Johan Heldenbergh, the film has a very American mood and almost won an Oscar.

469 **OFFLINE**

Peter Monsaert's 2013 film *Offline* tells the story of a man who leaves prison after seven years and tries to return to his old job repairing washing machines, but finally realises that this is impossible. Filmed in Ghent, it is a powerful, raw drama with strong Flemish actors and a dark soundtrack by the Belgian band Triggerfinger.

470 **MOSCOW, BELGIUM**

Christophe Van Rompaey's 2008 romantic drama *Aanrijding in Moscou* tells the story of Matty, a stressed Belgian mother living in the Ghent suburb of Moscou. She begins a stormy relationship with a truck driver after crashing into his truck outside a supermarket car park. The film was mostly shot in Ledeberg, but takes its title from a place where Russian troops camped before the Battle of Waterloo.

The 5 strangest
STREET NAMES

---

471 REGINALD WARNEFORDSTRAAT

Reginald Warneford-
straat
Dampoort ⑧

Not many people know the story behind this street name. It commemorates a dashing British pilot in the First World War who shot down a German Zeppelin as it flew over Ghent on 7 June 1915. The burning airship crashed onto the street now called Reginald Warnefordstraat. The pilot died just ten days later in a plane crash.

472 FACEBOOKSTEEG

Boeksteeg
Central Ghent ①

A narrow alley called Boeksteeg (Book Lane) runs down from Veldstraat to the River Leie. A second sign attached to the wall gives the street name as Facebooksteeg. This unofficial street sign was put up by the artists Har Hollands and Kees Bos during the Ghent Light Festival in 2012.

473 KINDERRECHTEN PLEIN

Lievekaai
Patershol ②

A cobbled square next to the River Lieve was temporarily renamed Kinderrechtenplein (Children's Rights Square) on 19 November 1999. The street signs are still there, but the name doesn't appear on any city map.

474 **PLEIN TEGEN ZINLOOS GEWELD**

Korenmarkt
Central Ghent ①

The street name on the former post office building on Korenmarkt reads Plein Tegen Zinloos Geweld (Square against Senseless Violence). The sign was put up in 2011 by an organisation that campaigns against violence.

475 **ZONDER-NAAMSTRAAT**

Zonder-Naamstraat
Dampoort ⑧

No one can explain this puzzling street name in northern Ghent. It means, literally, No Name Street.

475 ZONDER-NAAMSTRAAT

474 PLEIN TEGEN ZINLOOS GEWELD

The 5 best
RELICS OF THE 1913 WORLD FAIR

476 SINT-PIETERS-STATION
Koningin Maria
Hendrikaplein
Station Quarter ⑦

A stunning new railway station was built in southern Ghent in 1909-13, close to the site of the 1913 World Fair. The aim was to persuade visitors that Ghent was every bit as mediaeval as Bruges. Designed by Louis Croquet in Flemish mediaeval style, it is adorned with turrets, a clock tower and mock mediaeval frescoes. It is worth pausing a moment in the main booking hall to look up at the spectacular murals representing 13 Belgian cities.

477 DEN ENGHEL
Graslei 8
Central Ghent ①

The houses along the Graslei canal were carefully restored in 1913 to recreate the look of a mediaeval city. But there was a gap at No. 8 which was eventually filled by reconstructing the vanished Guild House of the Masons using old architectural plans. But then the original house was discovered during building work in 1976. It can be seen, five minutes' walk from here, at Cataloniëstraat.

476 SINT-PIETERSSTATION

478 FLANDRIA PALACE

Koningin Maria
Hendrikaplein
Station Quarter ⑦

The huge Flandria Hotel was built opposite Sint-Pietersstation to accommodate international visitors to the World Fair. With its 1,000 rooms, it was the largest hotel in the city. The grand building is now occupied by the offices of Belgian Railways.

479 SIRE VAN MALDEGHEM COLUMN

Sint-Veerleplein
Central Ghent ①

Take a look at the stone column in the square opposite the Gravensteen. It looks a relic of the Middle Ages, but the inscription reveals that it was placed here in 1926 by *les amis du vieux Gand*, the friends of Old Ghent, in memory of the people who brought the World Fair to Ghent. The design is based on a set of four vanished 15th-century columns that were placed at the corners of this square by an aristocrat called Sire Gheleyn van Maldeghem.

480 ROS BEIAARD STATUE

Paul de Smet de
Naeyerplein
Station Quarter ⑦

A strange statue survives from the 1913 World Fair in a small park behind the station. The Ros Beiaard statue represents a mediaeval Flemish legend in which a miraculous horse carried four brothers across Europe.

The 5 most creative
GHENT BANDS

481 ABSYNTHE MINDED
absyntheminded.be

Bert Ostyn started out in 1999 recording songs in a tiny bedroom in Ghent. He later joined up with four other musicians to form the band Absynthe Minded, who play gentle rock songs tinged with melancholy. Listen to the track *Space*.

482 KING DALTON
www.kingdalton.be

King Dalton started out playing on quiet Sunday nights in the Ghent café Charlatan. Slowly they developed a strange sound that they call avant-garde folk blues. They have created several catchy songs such as *Diligence*.

483 DAS POP
www.daspop.com

Das Pop was founded by four school students in Ghent. They began by playing to small audiences in scruffy Ghent bars and eventually scored a hit with the 2008 single *Fool for Love*. They now perform in major concert venues and summer festivals across Europe.

484 BALTHAZAR

www.balthazarband.be

This indie quintet was formed in 2004 by two buskers from Ghent. They have slowly built up a following in northern Europe with quiet melodies that flow along gently. It took them until 2010 to bring out their first album *Applause*. The second album Rates followed a couple of years later. Listen to the 2014 single *Leipzig*.

485 BINTI

Six sisters from Ghent with Egyptian roots have evolved a unique sound that mixes blues, barbershop, reggae and soul. They can sometimes be heard performing in small Ghent venues. Listen to *It's You*.

The 5 best
FEMALE SINGERS

---

486 SARAH FERRI
www.sarahferri.be

Her father is Italian. Her mother is Belgian. Sarah Ferri sings jazzy songs in a fiery gypsy voice. She belongs in a smoky bar in Havana, but for the moment she performs in small venues in Ghent, Brussels and Amsterdam. Listen to *Dancing at the Supermarket*.

487 LOVE LIKE BIRDS
lovelikebirds. wordpress.com

Elke De Mey is a young Ghent woman who sings aching folk songs in a soft, haunting voice. She performs in English in small Belgian venues, usually with guitar and piano backing. Her first album contained just five songs, but each one was perfect. Listen to *Heavy Heart to hear* what she can do with her voice.

488 TRIXIE WHITLEY

www.trixiewhitley.com

Born in Ghent, Trixie Whitley was the daughter of a blues singer called Chris Whitley. She grew up in Ghent and New York in a restless artistic family. She looks frail and damaged, but sings dark, powerful songs in a deep, emotional voice. Listen to *A Thousand Thieves* and *Breathe you in my dreams*.

489 AN PIERLÉ

www.anpierle.be

An Pierlé recorded her first album in a church attic in Ghent in 1998. Titled Mud Stories, it featured bare, haunting songs accompanied by piano. Pierlé has gone on to captivate listeners with her beautiful, tender melodies and quiet piano playing. Listen to *Strange Days*.

490 RENÉE

www.reneemusic.be

Renée Sys began to gather fans in 2012 when she released an album of tender love songs. She lives in Drongen castle outside Ghent where some of her video clips are filmed. Listen to *Dum Dum Dum*.

The 5 best
CYCLE TRIPS
from Ghent

---

491 DOWN THE LEIE TO AFSNEE

Bijlokekaai
Bijloke Quarter ③
FOLLOW NUMBERS
4, 52, 56, 62, 63, 61, 58, 57, 52, 4
www.fietsnet.be
www.fietsroute.org

Not many people take a bike out of Ghent, yet it is surprisingly easy to reach peaceful countryside by following one of the cycle paths that run next to rivers and canals. Our favourite escape route follows the River Leie past the STAM museum and the Blaarmeersen sport park. You are soon out in the countryside following a quiet river path that brings you eventually to a ferry. Here you can cross the river (if the ferry is operating) to reach the village of Afsnee, where you find a bike-friendly café near the ferry. Now you head through meadows and across a curious suspension bridge to reach Drongen abbey. It's worth buying a Ghent cycle map or checking your route on the fietsroute cycling website. You can then work out your route using the system of numbered bike signs known as *knooppunten*.

492 SINT-MARTENS-LATEM

Jozef Plateaustraat
University Quarter ⑥
FOLLOW NUMBERS
4, 2, 30, 88, 67, 63, 56, 52, 4
www.fietsnet.be
www.fietsroute.org

Head south from Vooruit through the Citadelpark and the elegant southern suburbs to reach Zwijnaarde. You can then follow narrow country lanes through watery meadows and woods to reach the village of Sint-Martens Latem. Continue to Afsnee, where you can stop at a cyclist-friendly café, before heading back to Ghent.

493 DOWN THE SCHELDT TO ZWIJNAARDE

Jozef Plateaustraat
University Quarter ⑥
FOLLOW NUMBERS
4, 5, 3, 40, 32, 29, 41, 97,
98, 99, 1, 3, 5, 4
www.fietsnet.be
www.fietsroute.org

One easy cycling route follows the quiet Visserij waterfront and then continues south to Ledeberg. Several bridges and underpasses carry cyclists safely across three motorways. But once you are in Zwijnaarde, you simply follow the traffic-free Schelde towpath until you come to a bridge. On the other side, you can follow a hilly route through cobbled lanes with almost no traffic back toward Zwijnaarde.

494 DOWN THE SCHELDT TO MELLE

Citadellaan/Visserij
University Quarter ⑥
FOLLOW NUMBERS
5, 7, 12, 22, 66, 28, 24, 21,
22, 12, 7, 5
www.fietsnet.be
www.fietsroute.org

You find a well-marked cycle route to the south of the university quarter that follows the banks of the River Scheldt. You can cycle to Melle and then head across the meadows to the village of Laarne before heading back by the Scheldt into Ghent.

495 ALONG THE GHENT-BRUGES CANAL

Coupure Links
Bijloke Quarter ③
FOLLOW NUMBERS
4, 50, 51, 54, 55, 46, 60, 65,
61, 58, 57, 52, 4
www.fietsnet.be
www.fietsroute.org

The Coupure canal offers another easy route out of town to the village of Vinderhoute where you pass close to several castles. You then cycle through flat Flemish farmland to arrive at the village of Drongen where you can stop at a café before heading back into Ghent.

The 5 people who have
MADE GHENT COOL

496 **WALTER DE BUCK**

Ghent would not be the same place without the bearded folk singer Walter De Buck. He helped to set up the artists' café Trefpunt in 1962 and turned the Gentse Feesten from a shabby funfair into Europe's largest music and street theatre festival. He has also created several strange sculptures that are dotted around the city.

497 **JAN HOET**

Jan Hoet created one of the most innovative art events ever seen in Belgium in 1986 when he exhibited contemporary art in 50 private homes across Ghent. His initiative put the city on the map as a centre for innovative modern art in unusual locations.

498 FRANK BEKE

As socialist mayor of Ghent from 1995 to 2006, Frank Beke was behind several inspiring urban projects, such as the creation of an extensive car-free zone in 1996. He was an immensely popular mayor who helped to turn an ailing industrial city into a warm and innovative place to live.

499 SOULWAX

The brothers David and Stephen Dewaele are the talented musicians behind the electronic band Soulwax. They also perform under the name 2ManyDJs and occasionally do gigs as Radio Soulwax. They are credited with inventing the mashup in 2001 when they released the album *As Heard on Radio Soulwax Pt. 2*, which blended 45 different tracks. Listen to: *This is Belgium Part One*.

500 BUÉ THE WARRIOR

Bué the Warrior comes from a long line of illustrators. Both his father and grandfather illustrated Belgian comic strips working in the Vandersteen studio. But Bué went in a different direction in 1991 when he started spraying walls with smiley cartoon characters. His work has brightened up many blank walls around the city and helped to turn Ghent into a destination for street art fans.

INDEX

COLOPHON

EDITING *and* **COMPOSING** – Derek Blyth
GRAPHIC DESIGN – Joke Gossé
PHOTOGRAPHY – Joram Van Holen en Jonas Mertens

The author and publisher wish to thank the following people, who were consulted regarding the selection of the addresses in this book: Koen Phlips, Melanie Devrieze, Nathalie Dumon, Amaury Van Kenhove, Bart Van Aken, Gudrun Rombaut, Fredo De Smet, Hilde Peleman.

The addresses in this book have been selected after thorough independent research by the author, in collaboration with Luster Publishers. The selection is solely based on personal evaluation of the business by the author. Nothing in this book was published in exchange for payment or benefits of any kind.

D/2014/12.005/5
ISBN 978 94 6058 1229
NUR 506

© 2014, Luster, Antwerp
Second, updated edition, February 2015
www.lusterweb.com
info@lusterweb.com

Printed in Belgium (Bruges) by Die Keure.